WORDSWORTH CLASSICS
OF WORLD LITERATURE

General Editor: Tom Griffith MA, MPhil

THE ANALECTS

Confucius

The Analects

Translated with Notes by Arthur Waley
With an Introduction by Robert Wilkinson

WORDSWORTH CLASSICS
OF WORLD LITERATURE

This edition published 1996 by Wordsworth Editions Limited
Cumberland House, Crib Street, Ware, Hertfordshire SG12 9ET

ISBN 1 85326 462 8

Typeset in Great Britain by Antony Gray
Printed and bound in Denmark by Nørhaven

The paper in this book is produced from pure wood
pulp, without the use of chlorine or any other substance
harmful to the environment. The energy used in its
production consists almost entirely of hydroelectricity
and heat generated from waste material, thereby
conserving fossil fuels and contributing little
to the greenhouse effect.

PREFATORY NOTE

Two systems for the romanisation of Chinese are currently in use in the West, one of Western origin – the Wade-Giles system – and the other, more recent and introduced by the Chinese themselves, called *pinyin*. Some currently available translations of and commentaries on Confucius use one system and some the other, making cross-reference occasionally confusing for non-specialists. To offset this difficulty, the following convention is observed in the Introduction. The translation printed in this book uses the Wade-Giles system, and therefore key Chinese terms are given in that romanisation. At their first occurrence, however, the *pinyin* equivalent is given in square brackets immediately after the Wade-Giles version. For example, the name of the great Chinese historian of the first century BC is given as Ssu-ma Ch'ien [Sima Qian] and his work as *Shih Chi* [*Shiji*] (*Historical Records*). In about one third of cases, the two systems give the same romanisation, and therefore in these instances one form only appears at the first occurrence of the word concerned.

INTRODUCTION

It is difficult to think of a philosopher in the history of Western civilisation who has a place of such centrality as Confucius in that of China. Until the fall of the Chinese Empire in 1911, the moral and political ideals attributed to Confucius informed every aspect of Chinese life, and a thorough knowledge of his ideas was one of the unquestioned preconditions for the achievement of the goal of every ambitious Chinese, an appointment in the civil service. Again, he is one of only two Chinese philosophers, from a long and very rich tradition of thought, to be known sufficiently well in the West to have attracted a Latinised form of his name: to the Chinese, Confucius is K'ung Fu-tzu [Kong fuzi], the Master K'ung. (The other philosopher whose name has been Latinised is Mencius, 371–289 BC, the second great Confucian philosopher. In Chinese, his name is Meng K'e.) K'ung Fu-tzu is certainly the only philosopher of world class so well known as to be referable to in Hollywood movies, albeit (generally) in the context of grossly simplistic and patronising depictions of things Chinese. It is very unlikely that all this could occur without good cause: a set of beliefs so durable, so influential and so widely known must in some special way be remarkable.

Of Master K'ung himself it is not possible to say a great deal with certainty: even the traditional dates for his birth and death, 551 and 479 BC, are probably not entirely accurate, since it was not the custom of the ancient Chinese to extend precise dating beyond the sphere of public events. Again, there is a biography of him in the *Shih-chi* [*Shiji*] (*Historical Records*) of Ssu-ma Ch'ien [Sima Qian] (145–c.86 BC), the greatest of all Chinese historical works, but a glance at the dates will show that Ssu-ma was writing some four hundred years after the Master's lifetime, and by then a nimbus of legend and hagiographic addition had long since gathered around his name. The most commonly held beliefs about his life are as follows: the Master was born in the state of Lu (now Shantung) and lived during the Chou [Zhou] dynasty (c.1025–256 BC). He is said to have had an elderly father who died when his son was young, and thereafter to have been brought up in humble circumstances by his mother. He attained modest public office, and hoped to attain a position of influence in politics, but the circumstances of the time were against him. The early years of the Chou dynasty had been characterised by political unity and so strength under the kings Wen and Wu (to whom, as will be seen, the Master constantly refers as models). By the time of K'ung's life however, this was no longer the case, and the dynasty had been greatly weakened by both internal squabbling and attacks from other states and barbarians. The state of Lu itself was under the control of usurpers and, unable to obtain a suitable post, K'ung spent the latter part of his life as a wandering teacher, moving from state to state and court to court, accompanied by a few disciples, offering his services as moral and political adviser.

It might be assumed that a somewhat safer source of information about the Master is the text of the *Analects* itself, but even here it is necessary to be cautious. The Chinese title of this text is *Lun yü* [*Lun yu*] meaning 'selected sayings' (more nearly preserved in the usual French rendering, *entretiens*). However, the title 'analects' given to his English version by one of its earlier translators, James Legge (in 1861), gives a hint as to one of the major areas of difficulty. 'Analects', from the Latin *analecta* (one who collects crumbs after a meal) and the Greek verb *analegein* (to gather together) means 'literary gleanings': what we have in the text is a set of short sayings, very few longer than half a dozen lines, written down some time after the Master's death and subject to the vagaries of early editors and the accidents of time. How much of what is now accepted as the authentic text was composed at one time relatively soon after K'ung's death is a matter of dispute among scholars. If one pays heed to internal consistency of doctrine, then Books III–IX and XI–XV inclusive are the most reliable sections of the text. Books I and II are much less orderly in their arrangement, and Book X, though not logically inconsistent in content with Books III–IX, appears to be an interpolation, consisting as it does not of moral philosophy but of a set of rules concerning the rites, a notion to which we will return. Again, Book XIX consists entirely of sayings of disciples, and in other places (e.g. XVI, 14;

XVIII, 9–11; XX, 1) stray paragraphs from other texts have manifestly found their way to a place where they do not belong.

However, from the more reliable sections of this ancient text emerges a consistent philosophy. The Master's aim in formulating his ideas was no less than to devise a set of moral and political beliefs which, if widely and consistently acted on in human society, would produce the greatest good of which he could conceive, namely a stable social and political order in which human beings could flourish, a condition very different from the one he saw around him. As has been the case throughout the history of Chinese thought – and as is still true today in a China officially Marxist – this philosophy is no mere arabesque of concepts spun by a detached thinker in a sheltered and privileged situation. It is intended to be a working solution to some of the most urgent human concerns: to identify the nature of moral goodness, and to trace its implications in both private morality and the theory of government.

The approach taken by the Master in addressing these issues is to a degree similar to that adopted by Aristotle in his *Nicomachean Ethics* and constitutes what philosophers term a 'virtue ethic': the moral philosophy is cast as a description of ideal characters, characterised via a set of moral virtues in which moral goodness is held to consist, and in the Master's case a description of how these virtues would manifest themselves if applied in the arena of politics. K'ung assumes, as does Aristotle, that by and large whether we become morally upright and govern well is up to us, but he has to acknowledge that, however well we behave and lay our plans, we are at times at the mercy of forces over which we have no control. To these he refers as *t'ien* [*tian*] (Heaven) and *ming* (Fate or Destiny), both rendered here by Waley as 'Heaven'. Neither term is defined by the Master, nor are they used systematically differently, though there is a hint that *ming* denotes an entirely impersonal Destiny without any hint of purposiveness or agency even by superhuman agents (as also in the *Mencius*, V, A, 6): this is the idea present in VI, 2 where the Master speaks regretfully of the short life span allocated to his disciple Yen Hui [Yan Hui] by Heaven (cf. XIV, 38). By contrast, in other remarks, 'Heaven' appears to be used to denote a feature more akin to providence in Christian thought, a purposive force which intervenes in history, altering the direction of human affairs: thus (VII, 22), K'ung speaks of Heaven as the source of his power. By his use of these terms, the Master is acknowledging, entirely realistically, that there are occasions when large features of the order of things simply alter, mocking our tiny purposes, and there is nothing we can do about it. This acknowledgement made, the Master does not further concern himself with other-worldly matters, either in respect of Heaven or of ghosts and spirits. He never spoke of the latter (VII, 20), and evidently regarded concern with them as a waste of time, a deflection from the more pressing and less speculative business of dealing with the living (XI, 11; cf. VI, 20). The philosophy of the *Analects* is firmly focused on this world, not the next.

As indicated above, Confucius was not a fatalist, and the bulk of what he has to say is devoted to describing moral ideals. Many moral and religious thinkers, in both East and West, include in their philosophy an ultimate moral ideal at the very limit of human powers of attainment. For example, the great philosopher Immanuel Kant (1724–1804) describes what he terms the person possessed of a 'holy will': this is a person whose spontaneous actions accord perfectly with the moral law. For most of us most of the time doing our duty and fulfilling our obligations is something we find an effort or a burden, since it generally involves us in thwarting the desires of our own ego and putting others first: hence we need the apparatus of moral schooling and cultivation, which both Kant and Confucius, in their different ways, describe. By contrast, the person of holy will feels no burden of duty and has no need to be schooled, since the unfettered impulses of such a person are in perfect accord with the demands of morality. Kant would not have expected to be able to find such a person, and this is also true of Confucius and the ideal figure which corresponds in his thought to Kant's person of holy will, namely the Divine Sage, *sheng* or *sheng jen* [*sheng ren*]. He denied that he himself was one (VIII, 31), and says he could never even hope to meet one (VII, 25). The Sage would be able not only to bring benefits to the common people, but also to save an entire state (VI, 28); in common with other Confucian ideals, sagehood is not reclusive, and is manifested in the arena of politics as well as private morality.

Though the Master could not hope to meet a Sage, he could hope to meet the ideal type most fully described in the *Analects*, the *chün tzu* [*junzi*] or gentleman: the gentleman in Confucius's thought occupies a position analogous to that of the philosopher-kings in the ideal state described in Plato's *Republic*: were the state run by gentlemen, all would be well for reasons which will become clear below. The gentleman is described in terms of the set of virtues which he possesses: he exhibits a certain gravitas (necessary if he is to keep the respect of inferiors); he keeps his promises; he is loyal to his superiors and is not afraid to admit to his own errors and correct them (I, 8). He is always concerned to do what is right, *yi*, not simply with what is profitable (the profit motive was regarded with contempt) (IV, 16), and, though cultivated, never parades his cultivation to the extent of infringing the received standards of behaviour codified in the rites (VI, 25). The rites or ritual, *li*, were the manners and forms of correct behaviour, and the many examples in Book X of the *Analects* show what the Master had in mind, e.g. 'When saluting his colleagues he passes his right hand to the left, letting his robe hang down in front and behind; and as he advances with quickened step, his attitude is one of majestic dignity' (X, 3). The concept of rites or manners in this sense is one familiar to us all: we in the West have forms of dress, speech and demeanour which are regarded as appropriate in civilised society. We dress differently for weddings, funerals, interviews, court appearances, and the like, than we do for our leisure and much of our work time. Forms of address to strangers are different from those to friends, and so on. These customs have evolved for a number of reasons, for example to avoid friction and disorder, to show respect, or to mark out some events as special and standing out from the usual, the humdrum and the routine. Though the rites of the ancient Chinese were more extensive and closely specified than our own, they had precisely the same functions and were no less, and no more, arbitrary. Interestingly, though he respected it greatly (XII, 1), the Master did not advocate slavish adherence to the letter of ritual: he considered the intention behind the custom, and only followed the specified usage unswervingly if he concluded that the custom embodied an attitude or distinction which was morally significant (IX, 3).

There is a close link between observing the rites and most important of all Confucian virtues, *jen* [*ren*] (cf. XII, 2). In the present translation it is rendered as 'Goodness' and in others as 'perfect virtue', 'humaneness', 'human-heartedness' or 'benevolence'. What these differences among translators, all of whom are expert, indicate is an important non-alignment between the concepts we use and those of the ancient Chinese: there is no single concept in our moral vocabulary which captures precisely what the Master means by *jen*.

'Goodness' and 'perfect virtue' have the merit of indicating correctly that *jen* is the supreme virtue in the Master's thought, while 'humaneness', 'benevolence' and so on give a flavour of the precise form of goodness he had in mind. The person who has *jen* loves others (XII, 22), shows 'Courtesy, breadth, good faith, diligence and clemency' (XVII, 6), is never glib or pretentious (I, 3) and is courageous (XIV, 5: the Master points out, however, that though the Good are always courageous, those with courage, *yung* [*yong*], need not necessarily be Good). There are two ways of working out what a Good person would do in any given situation: one way is to follow the prescribed rites, which, it can be assumed, are a codification of what a person with *jen* would do (XII, 1). Alternatively, we have only to look within ourselves: the Good person follows the rule, 'Do not do to others what you would not like yourself' (XII, 2; cf. XV, 23). This principle, elsewhere referred to as consideration, *shu*, was regarded as so central by the Master that he describes it, together with loyalty, *chung* [*zhong*], as the theme which unifies his whole outlook (IV, 15). From it an important consequence follows, namely that Goodness is not a remote or mysterious notion: 'Is Goodness indeed so far away? If we really wanted Goodness, we should find that it was at our very side' – i.e. because we need only examine ourselves in order to determine what is the correct course of action (VII, 29). The gentleman has *jen* to a high degree (IV, 5).

The gentleman also exhibits filial piety or respect for parents, *hsiao* [*xiao*], and respect for elder brothers, *t'i* [*ti*] (I, 2; I, 11; II, 5; II, 6–8). The fundamental obligation to one's parents is so to behave as never to give them cause for anxiety (II, 6). This does not mean that they can never be disagreed with or their views questioned, thought it does entail ultimate submission if they are unwilling to change their views (IV, 18). Obligations to parents extend after their death, when they should be mourned for the period stipulated in the rites (three years, cf. I, 11; II, 5; IV, 20). Confucius believed further that anyone who behaved well within the family would be likely to behave well in the public domain: a good son and a good brother can be relied on to be a good citizen (I, 2).

The acquisition of these virtues requires constant effort, to which the Master refers as *hsüeh* [*xue*], nearly always translated, as here, as 'learning'. However, as is the case with *jen,* the conceptual non-alignment between ancient Chinese and modern English makes it all but impossible to find a word in the latter language which means quite what *hsüeh* means. The Master does not mean that we should seek to become learned in the sense of amassing a great deal of book-learning without practical application, and even less would he applaud pedantry (cf. VI, 16). What he means is rather that we study for the sake of improving our moral insight and character, which in practical terms means the study of morally exemplary persons. Since, as we have seen, the Master did not find these around him in his lifetime, he finds his exemplars in the past, in the early Chou rulers. Learning is referred to frequently throughout the *Analects*, from I, 1 onwards. Not only is a love of learning essential for any person wishing to be a gentleman, but it is an area in which the usually modest Master claimed, for once, a degree of pre-eminence: he set his heart upon learning early, at the age of fifteen (II, 4), and doubted if many could be found who were as devoted to learning as himself (V, 27; cf. VII, 1–3).

It is important to stress that this learning is, as we would now put it, non-technical and non-vocational. Much as was the case until quite recently with the classics-based education thought essential for the English gentleman, the aim of the type of learning advocated by Confucius is a general intellectual and moral competence. As he remarks, 'A gentleman is not an implement' (II, 12), by which he means that the gentleman does not trouble himself with knowledge of specialist disciplines, like medicine or agriculture. Such specialist knowledge is regarded as a hindrance (XIX, 4). In his public role as official, the gentleman must have knowledge of how human beings behave (XII, 22), but that is as near to a 'specialism' as can be countenanced.

The Master further describes the gentleman as one 'who associates with those that possess the Way' (I, 14). The Way is the *Tao* [*Dao*]; this term is relatively familiar to Westerners as part of the title of the great Taoist classic the *Tao te ching* [*Dao de jing*] (*The Way and its Power*) and via its Japanese form *do*, frequently used as part of the name of particular disciplines or practices, martial or spiritual or both, e.g. *kendo; aikido; bushido; chado,* and so on. It is important to be clear, however, that this flexible concept is not used in the Taoist sense in the *Analects*. In the *Tao te ching*, the *Tao* is the ultimate reality, immutable, eternal and indescribable, behind (so to speak) the multifariousness of ordinary experience. Any such metaphysic is absent from the *Analects*. In this work, the Way is the way or path of principle or moral goodness which we should at all costs seek to follow in both our public and our private life. Anyone who grasps the Way has grasped the most important feature of the universe. 'The Master said, In the morning, hear the Way; in the evening, die content!' (IV, 8). The nearest analogue in Western thought to *Tao* I know of is the ancient Greek concept *logos,* which can mean not only 'word' but also 'principle' and in some cases the ultimate reality or god, as in the first verse of St John's Gospel. Both terms can be used to denote not only specific sets of organising principles but also the one principle behind the whole order of things.

Equally difficult to render into English is the term *te* [*de*]. A number of translators render this as 'virtue', but stress that it is necessary to be clear that this term does not have in this text its commonest current English sense, that in which it is the contrary of vice. Rather, it blends together a number of important connotations: it can simply mean 'virtue' in the sense of 'specific property', as in the English phrases, 'this has lost its virtue' or 'in virtue of '; further, when applied to persons, it connotes what we might now call character, the outward manifestation of a certain inner force. Again, it is clear that the Master regarded *te* as Heaven-sent (VII, 22), importantly different in this respect from *jen.* In the face of these complexities, the translator of the present text opted to use several different English terms to render *te,* the most frequently used being 'moral force'. The term *te* has been retained in brackets in the text to indicate where other English words have been used to translate it.

Following the way is an attribute not only of the gentleman but also of those who fell into the class of *shih* [*shi*], a term rendered by Waley as 'knight'. Once again, a comparison with other translations reveals some seemingly startlingly different renderings, e.g. 'scholar', 'officer', 'serviceman' or 'public servant', and, as in the other cases noted above, what lies behind this variety is the impossibility of finding any neat English equivalent term for the class of people of whom the Master is speaking, the case being further complicated by the change in sense of this term over time. The best opinion at present is that, when the Master was alive, the *shih* were minor aristocrats dispossessed by political circumstance of their inheritance and forced to earn a living by taking public office of some kind. (In later times, the *shih* were the literati or gentleman-scholars who had passed the civil service examinations and who were employed in the administration.) In the

Analects, Confucius is concerned to set out the ideal character such a person should possess and is thereby specifying the character appropriate for those holding public office: straightforward and a lover of right (XII, 20); more concerned with the Way than with personal comfort and vanities (IV, 9); and scrupulous in not putting his own interests ahead of following the path of duty (XIII, 20).

The gentleman and the knight constitute the attainable moral ideals in the Master's outlook. They are contrasted with the *hsiao-jen* [*xiao ren*], literally the small man, a term rendered in a number of different ways by Waley: e.g. 'small man' (II, 14), 'commoner' (IV, 11), 'lesser man' (IV, 16), 'small people' (XII, 19), 'common people' (XIV, 26). The *hsiao-jen* is the person who does not have *jen* and who does not behave in a morally principled manner. The lack of moral principle manifests itself in various forms of egotism but principally as greed: while the gentleman does what is right, the small or lesser man only considers what is profitable (IV, 16). Again the small man tries to dodge any punishment or sanction he may have merited (IV, 11), having no respect for impersonal operation of moral or legal principle. Such a person is incapable of impartiality: a gentleman can see all sides of a question; the small man sees only his own interest and is therefore always biased (II, 14 cf. XII, 16). People who are relentlessly concerned with satisfying their own wants and desires are invariably unquiet, since they live in constant fear of being thwarted: hence, with exact moral psychology, the Master notes that while the gentleman is calm, the small man is fretful and ill at ease (VII, 36). Equally accurately, Confucius points out that those who are morally cultivated stand up to hardship much better than the *hsiao-jen*: to the small man, prolonged or serious non-satisfaction of egocentric desire is the worst situation imaginable, and in hard times such people tend to go to pieces, swept away by their own self-pity or panic (cf. XV, 1). The Master refers to the small man more than twenty times, and taken together, his remarks furnish a penetrating picture of a human type which has so far proved perennial and ubiquitous.

Such people have a damaging effect on the social order, and the surest way for this order to be strengthened is for gentlemen and knights to be in charge of government. What the small man cannot do is withstand the force of moral example: 'The essence of the gentleman is that of wind; the essence of small people is that of grass. And when a wind passes over the grass, it cannot choose but bend'

(XII, 19). One of the main themes of the *Analects* is the nature of good government, and the Master has a good deal to say about how rulers should conduct themselves, and about those who are governed. It is to be stressed at the outset that Confucius simply takes it as axiomatic that society can be divided into those fit to rule and those fit to be ruled. Forms of egalitarianism with which we are now familiar are quite absent from this text, as is any notion of democracy or consultation of the governed, even in the very limited form in which this was practised in the city-states of Greece in classical times. It follows that, somewhat as was believed in Great Britain until fairly recently, people have a station in life and role in society which it is necessary for them to fulfil if order is to be maintained, and this is the thought behind the Confucian doctrine known, not altogether happily, as 'the rectification of names': the prince must act as befits a prince; the minister as befits a minister; the father as befits a father; the son as befits a son (cf. XII, 11; XIII, 3). What is being advocated here is that people must fulfil the obligations appropriate to their social roles: their 'names' (labels specifying social roles) are 'rectified' if they act as they are supposed to, and so language and reality are in accord.

Those who are governed are the common people, *min,* and there can be no doubt that the Master's attitude to them as it emerges from the *Analects* was firmly paternalistic. The common people are of poor understanding: though they can be brought to act in accordance with the Way, they cannot grasp it (VIII, 9), and they find learning too difficult to undertake (XVI, 9). On the other hand, it follows from the ideal of *jen* and from the Master's other moral beliefs that the people ought to be treated with a certain consideration and certainly not just as beasts of burden and (so to speak) cannon fodder. They must have sufficient food (VII, 7), and should not be used for military service when they are needed in the fields (I, 5). Again, when they are needed for military service, they must be properly instructed beforehand (XIII, 29–30), and this instruction is principally moral instruction.

The sources of this moral instruction are the gentlemen and knights in their public capacity as rulers, administrators and officers. As was noted above, Confucian moral ideals are not reclusive, and the Master regarded it as obligatory (with a qualification to be noted below) for the gentleman to take public office. This view rests on one of the central presuppositions of the moral psychology of the *Analects*, namely that a morally exemplary character has the power to inspire respect and morally right conduct in others (the same belief also underlies much of what Confucius has to say about *hsüeh* or learning, where the objects of study are precisely the records of morally exemplary persons in both the private and the public sphere). Hence Confucius, asked about the art of ruling, insists that the first duty of the ruler is to deal uprightly with people (cf XII, 17; XIII, 6): such a mode of behaviour inspires respect and obedience in others, and is a much surer way of establishing authority than edict or threat (cf. XII, 19; XII, 22; II, 1; II, 19, 20). Again, if the rulers are Good, there will be no need to go to law to settle disputes, since the rule of the Good is always in accord with what is right (cf. XII, 13). Further, since the gentleman is unbiased, and impartial, he is not politically partisan: hence the saying that such a person 'allies himself with individuals, but not with parties' (XV, 21). No one will feel guilty about disobeying the commands of a ruler regarded as corrupt; but the moral authority of the Good man is absolute, even if the common people cannot intellectually grasp it (cf. VIII, 19). The effect of such a ruler is to benefit everyone (VI, 28).

As has been indicated, it would seem to follow from Confucius's premises that it is not only permissible but also obligatory for the gentleman to seek public office, and indeed he often speaks in this way (cf. XIX, 13). At other places in the text, however, the Master appears to suggest that a gentleman should take office only when the Way prevails in the state, as in the case of Ch'ü Po Yü [Qu Boyu], who is given the title 'gentleman': 'When the Way prevailed in his land, he served the State; but when the Way ceased to prevail, he knew how to wrap it [i.e. his talent] up and hide it in the folds of his dress' (XV, 6). The difficulty is compounded by the strength of the exemplary power the Master at times attributes to the conduct of the gentleman, e.g. he is credited with the ability to civilise barbarians (IX, 13; cf. XIII, 12). These positions can perhaps be reconciled if one adopts the extended sense of the term 'government' used in II, 21, where the Master, asked why he is not himself in public office, quotes in reply the statement: 'Be filial, only be filial and friendly towards your brothers, and you will be contributing to government'; but this is not entirely convincing. It is quite possible that the Master changed his mind on this point, but this is only speculation. The remarks collected in the *Analects* have no context, and it is impossible to glean from them any hint of a development in the Master's thought.

Such in outline are the leading ideas put forward in the *Analects*, and it would be difficult to overestimate their importance both for Chinese philosophy in particular and Chinese civilisation in general. With regard to the former, Confucianism became one of the three major traditions in China (the other two being Taoism and Buddhism), and the *Analects* furnished the starting point for a number of major philosophers who added to or reinterpreted the ideas of the Master – this is a pattern followed repeatedly in major philosophical traditions, not only in the West, where, for example, the ideas of Plato and Aristotle have been a source and inspiration for philosophers ever since, but also in India. (The scattered insights of the *Upanishads*, for example, were systematised into the philosophy of the *Brahma Sutra* (2nd century BC), which itself then inspired a long line of major philosophers.) In China, the process cf the interpretation and amplification of Confucianism begins with Mencius (371–289 BC). One of the important areas of moral philosophy on which no significant remarks by Confucius have survived and where consequently there is a gap to be filled is the issue of whether there is anything useful to be said about human nature in general: in both East and West, philosophers have expressed a spectrum of opinions on this point, ranging from those who regard human beings as fundamentally wicked and so in need of discipline, via those who think there is no pre-existent human nature at all, to those who believe human beings are basically benign and only corrupted by force of circumstance. Mencius took the view that there is at least a degree of innate goodness in human nature, and argues for this on the basis of empirical observation: 'Suppose a man were, all of a sudden, to see a young child on the verge of falling into a well. He would certainly be moved to compassion, not because he wanted to get in the good graces of the parents, nor because he wished to win the praise of his fellow villagers or friends, nor yet because he disliked the cry of the child. The heart of compassion is the germ of benevolence.' (*Mencius* II, A, 6; D. C. Lau's version. Those familiar with Western philosophy will note the similarity of these views to those of Hume, e.g. *Enquiry Concerning the Principles of Morals* (1751), Appendix II.)

This is in direct contrast to the beliefs on this point advanced by the third great Confucian philosopher Hsün Tzu [Xunzi], born around 312 BC. Hsün's view of human nature is much more like that of Hobbes: 'Man's nature is evil, goodness is the result of conscious activity, any man who follows his nature and indulges his emotions will violate the forms and rules of society, and will end as a criminal' (*Hsün Tzu,* section 23, Burton Watson's version), i.e. we are naturally inclined to all the forms of selfishness, and only attain to moral conduct if properly trained. Examples like this could be multiplied, and significant philosophical developments took place in this tradition over many centuries, reaching to the neo-Confucianism of Tai Chen [Dai Zhen] in the eighteenth century. A tradition of this kind only comes about when the seminal ideas are of the greatest penetration, and is a testimony to the profundity of the leading ideas of the *Analects.*

Though there are fairly direct Western analogues to the influence of a seminal philosopher within philosophy itself, no Western philosopher has influenced the spirit of an entire and very durable culture as did Confucius. The *Analects,* together with two other Confucian works, the *Great Learning* and the *Doctrine of the Mean,* together with the *Mencius,* became the Four Books which were the set texts for the all-important civil service examinations in Imperial China. Though it would be rash to say that the reality of Imperial China realised Confucian ideals any more closely than Communist China does those of Marx and Engels, these ideals were at least the recognised goals and standards for individual and state. That alone would be enough to guarantee Confucius a secure place in history, but it is to belittle his thought to attribute to it only historical interest, even on this scale. Perhaps the most astonishing feature of this ancient text is that, discounting the superficial accidents of cultural dress and manner, so to speak, the *Analects* speaks to us directly and incisively about questions we can understand. This is because Confucius is confronting issues on which we cannot plume ourselves on having made much progress: so long as humanity can devise no viable basic social unit other than the family, and so long as societies organise themselves into states, then Confucius's questions still stand. How should the members of families behave to one another? How should rulers behave? What sort of character is the ideal for human beings, both in the public and the private spheres? The answers Confucius gives are worthy of the greatest respect: his moral ideals are practicable and, as he saw, if they were followed by significant sections of the human race, our condition would, in a number of ways, be immeasurably improved.

ROBERT WILKINSON
Senior Lecturer in Philosophy
The Open University in Scotland

SUGGESTIONS FOR FURTHER READING

Other versions of the Analects
D. C. Lau (tr.), Harmondsworth, Penguin 1979
Raymond Dawson (tr.), Oxford World's Classics, Oxford University
   Press, Oxford 1993
J. Legge, *The Chinese Classics*, Volume I, Trubner, London 1861,
   and in later editions

On Chinese philosophy
Fung Yu-lan (tr. Derk Bodde), *A History of Chinese Philosophy*
   (2 vols), Princeton University Press, Princeton, Volume I (2nd
   edn), 1952, Vol II, 1953
Chan Wing-Tsit, *A Source Book in Chinese Philosophy*, Princeton
   University Press, Princeton 1963
D. Collinson and R. Wilkinson, *Thirty-Five Oriental Philosophers*,
   Routledge, London 1994

On Confucius
R. Dawson, *Confucius*, Oxford University Press, Oxford 1981
D. L. Hall, *Thinking Through Confucius*, State University of New
   York Press, Albany 1987
H. Fingarette, *Confucius: The Secular as Sacred*, Harper and Row,
   New York 1972

Other Confucian works referred to in the Introduction
J. Legge, *The Chinese Classics*, 'The Great Learning' and 'The Doc-
   trine of the Mean', Volume I, Trubner, London 1861, and later
   editions
Mencius (tr. D. C. Lau), Harmondsworth, Penguin 1970
Hsün Tzu (tr. Burton Watson), *Basic Writings*, Columbia University
   Press, New York and London 1963

On Imperial China
R. Dawson, *Imperial China*, Penguin, Harmondsworth 1972
I. Miyazaki (tr. Conrad Schirokauer), *China's Examination Hell*,
   Weatherhill, New York and Tokyo 1976

NOTE ON THE TEXT

The text printed here is that of the translation and notes by Arthur Waley, with the exception of notes referring to Waley's own introduction and to his detailed linguistic discussions of textual difficulties in the Chinese editions from which he worked.

Waley refers repeatedly in the notes to four Chinese works, which either pre-date or were contemporary with Confucius, and which were already classics in or about his time. They are usually referred to simply as 'the Classics'. They are:

1 *Shih Ching* [*The Book of Songs*], poems dating from the early Chou period. Waley refers to his own translation (London 1937; last reprinted Grove Press, New York 1987).

2 *Shu Ching* [*The Book of History*], records from 7000–2000 BC.

3 *I Ching* [*The Book of Changes*], a book of divination.

4 *Li Ching* [*The Book of Rites*], rules of conduct similar to those found in Book X of the *Analects*.

CONTENTS

THE ANALECTS

BOOK ONE

1   The Master said, To learn and at due times to repeat what one has learnt, is that not after all[1] a pleasure? That friends should come to one from afar,[2] is this not after all delightful? To remain unsoured even though one's merits are unrecognised by others, is that not after all what is expected of a gentleman?

2   Master Yu said, Those who in private life behave well towards their parents and elder brothers, in public life seldom show a disposition to resist the authority of their superiors. And as for such men starting a revolution, no instance of it has ever occurred. It is upon the trunk[3] that a gentleman works. When that is firmly set up, the Way grows. And surely proper behaviour towards parents and elder brothers is the trunk of Goodness?

3   The Master said, 'Clever talk and a pretentious manner'[4] are seldom found in the Good.

---

1   The 'after all' implies 'even though one does not hold office'.
2   Several of the disciples belonged to other States (e.g. Wei and Ch'i); but there is no evidence that they came to Lu on account of Confucius. Unless, however, there is here some allusion that escapes us, the phrase must refer to the visits of admirers from abroad, perhaps friends made during the Master's journeys in Honan.
3   i.e. upon what is fundamental, as opposed to 'the twigs', i.e. small arts and accomplishments, which the gentleman leaves to his inferiors.
4   Traditional phrase. cf. *Shu Ching*, Kao Yao Mo.

4   Master Tsêng said, Every day I examine myself on these three points: in acting on behalf of others, have I always been loyal to their interests? In intercourse with my friends, have I always been true to my word? Have I failed to repeat[1] the precepts that have been handed down to me?

5   The Master said, A country of a thousand war-chariots cannot be administered unless the ruler attends strictly to business, punctually observes his promises, is economical in expenditure, shows affection towards his subjects in general, and uses the labour of the peasantry only at the proper times of year.[2]

6   The Master said, A young man's duty is to behave well to his parents at home and to his elders abroad, to be cautious in giving promises and punctual in keeping them, to have kindly feelings towards everyone, but seek the intimacy of the Good. If, when all that is done, he has any energy to spare, then let him study the polite arts.[3]

7   Tzu-hsia said, A man who

> Treats his betters as betters,
> Wears an air of respect,
> Who into serving father and mother
> Knows how to put his whole strength,
> Who in the service of his prince will lay down his life,
> Who in intercourse with friends is true to his word –

others may say of him that he still lacks education,[4] but I for my part should certainly call him an educated man.

1   And so keep in memory.
2   i.e. not when they ought to be working in the fields. Bad rulers, on the contrary, listen to music or go hunting when they ought to be attending to business, continually employ labour on ostentatious building-schemes, etc.
3   i.e. learn to recite the *Songs*, practise archery, deportment, and the like.
4   i.e. knowledge of ritual, precedents, the correct use on social occasions of verse from the *Songs*, etc.

8 The Master said, If a gentleman is frivolous,[1] he will lose the respect of his inferiors and lack firm ground[2] upon which to build up his education. First and foremost he must learn to be faithful to his superiors, to keep promises, to refuse the friendship of all who are not like him.[3] And if he finds he has made a mistake, then he must not be afraid of admitting the fact and amending his ways.

9 Master Tsêng said, When proper respect towards the dead is shown at the End and continued after they are far away the moral force (te) of a people has reached its highest point.

10 Tzu-Ch'in[4] said to Tzu-kung, When our Master arrives in a fresh country he always manages to find out about its policy.[5] Does he do this by asking questions, or do people tell him of their own accord? Tzu-kung said, Our Master gets things by being cordial, frank, courteous, temperate, deferential. That is our Master's way of enquiring – a very different matter,[6] certainly, from the way in which enquiries are generally made.

11 The Master said, While a man's father is alive, you can only see his intentions; it is when his father dies that you discover whether or not he is capable of carrying them out. If for the whole three years of mourning he manages to carry on the household exactly as in his father's day, then he is a good son indeed.

1 i.e. irresponsible and unreliable in his dealings with others.
2 The sentence runs awkwardly and is probably corrupt.
3 i.e. of those who still reckon in terms of 'profit and loss', and have taken *jen* (Goodness) as standard.
4 Disciple of Confucius. See XVI, and XIX, 25.
5 Not, of course, about the details of administration, but about the secret, general maxims which inspire the ruler.
6 The double particle *ch'i-chu*, peculiar to the *Analects* and *Kungyang Chuan*, does not seem to differ in meaning from the ordinary modal *ch'i*.

12   Master Yu said, In the usages of ritual it is harmony[1] that is prized; the Way of the Former Kings from this[2] got its beauty. Both small matters and great depend upon it. If things go amiss, he who knows the harmony[3] will be able to attune them. But if harmony itself is not modulated by ritual, things will still go amiss.

13   Master Yu said,

> In your promises cleave to what is right,
> And you will be able to fulfil your word.
> In your obeisances cleave to ritual,
> And you will keep dishonour at bay.
> Marry one who has not betrayed her own kin,
> And you may safely present her to your Ancestors.[4]

14   The Master said, A gentleman who never goes on eating till he is sated, who does not demand comfort in his home, who is diligent in business and cautious in speech, who associates with those that possess the Way and thereby corrects his own faults – such a one may indeed be said to have a taste for learning.

15   Tzu-kung said, 'Poor without cadging, rich without swagger.' What of that?[5] The Master said, Not bad. But better still, 'Poor, yet delighting in the Way, rich, yet a student of ritual.' Tzu-kung said, The saying of the *Songs*,[6]

1   Harmony between man and nature; playing the musical mode that harmonises with the season, wearing seasonable clothes, eating seasonable food, and the like.
2   i.e. from harmony.
3   i.e. the act that harmonises with the moment.
4   Lines 2, 4, and 6 rhyme. For the last rhyme, which belongs to a well-established type, see Karlgren, *The Rimes in the Sung section of the Shi King*.
5   i.e. what of it as a motto?
6   *The Book of Songs* p. 46, which describes the elegance of a lover. Tzu-kung interprets it as describing the pains the gentleman has taken to improve his character, and suggests that Confucius prefers the second maxim ('Poor, yet delighting . . .') because it implies a greater effort of self-improvement.

> As thing cut, as thing filed,
> As thing chiselled, as thing polished

refers, I suppose, to what you have just said? The Master said, Ssu, now I can really begin to talk to you about the *Songs,* for when I allude to sayings of the past, you see what bearing they have on what was to come after.

16 The Master said, (The good man) does not grieve that other people do not recognise his merits. His only anxiety is lest he should fail to recognise theirs.

BOOK TWO

1   The Master said, He who rules by moral force (*te*) is like the pole-star, which remains in its place while all the lesser stars do homage to it.

2   The Master said, If out of the three hundred *Songs* I had to take one phrase to cover all my teaching, I would say 'Let there be no evil in your thoughts.'[1]

3   The Master said, Govern the people by regulations, keep order among them by chastisements, and they will flee from you, and lose all self-respect. Govern them by moral force, keep order among them by ritual and they will keep their self-respect and come to you of their own accord.

4   The Master said, At fifteen I set my heart upon learning. At thirty, I had planted my feet firm upon the ground. At forty, I no longer suffered from perplexities. At fifty, I knew what were the biddings of Heaven. At sixty, I heard them with docile ear. At seventy, I could follow the dictates of my own heart; for what I desired no longer overstepped the boundaries of right.

---

1   *The Book of Songs*, p. 275, l. 7, where however *ssu* does not mean 'thoughts', but is an exclamation, 'oh', 'ah', or the like; but in applying ancient texts it is the words themselves that matter, not the context; and these words can be reapplied in any sense which they are conceivably capable of bearing.

5   Mêng I Tzu[1] asked about the treatment of parents. The Master said, Never disobey! When Fan Ch'ih[2] was driving his carriage for him, the Master said, Mêng asked me about the treatment of parents and I said, Never disobey! Fan Ch'ih said, In what sense did you mean it? The Master said, While they are alive, serve them according to ritual. When they die, bury them according to ritual and sacrifice to them according to ritual.[3]

6   Mêng Wu Po[4] asked about the treatment of parents. The Master said, Behave in such a way that your father and mother have no anxiety about you, except concerning your health.

7   Tzu-Yu asked about the treatment of parents. The Master said, 'Filial sons' nowadays are people who see to it that their parents get enough to eat. But even dogs and horses are cared for to that extent. If there is no feeling of respect, wherein lies the difference?

8   Tzu-hsia asked about the treatment of parents. The Master said, It is the demeanour[5] that is difficult. Filial piety does not consist merely in young people undertaking the hard work, when anything has to be done, or serving their elders first with wine and food. It is something much more than that.

1   A young grandee of Lu, whose father sent him to study with Confucius. He died in 481 BC.
2   A disciple.
3   Evidently by 'disobey' Confucius meant 'disobey the rituals'. The reply was intended to puzzle the enquirer and make him think. In *Mencius*, III, A, 2, 'While they are alive . . .', etc., is given as a saying of Master Tsêng. Here and elsewhere 'sacrifice' means offerings in general and not only animal-sacrifice.
4   Son of Mêng I Tzu.
5   This is Chêng Hsüan's interpretation. Pao Hsien (6 BC–AD 65) takes *sê* to mean the expression of one's parents, which must be watched for hints of approval or disapproval.

9   The Master said, I can talk to Yen Hui[1] a whole day without his ever differing from me. One would think he was stupid. But if I enquire into his private conduct when he is not with me I find that it fully demonstrates what I have taught him. No, Hui is by no means stupid.

10 The Master said, Look closely into his aims, observe the means by which he pursues them, discover what brings him content – and can the man's real worth[2] remain hidden from you, can it remain hidden from you?

11 The Master said, He who by reanimating[3] the Old can gain knowledge of the New is fit to be a teacher.

12 The Master said, A gentleman is not an implement.[4]

13 Tzu-kung asked about the true gentleman. The Master said, He does not preach what he practises till he has practised what he preaches.

14 The Master said, A gentleman can see a question from all sides without bias. The small man is biased and can see a question only from one side.

1   The favourite disciple. His early death is several times referred to in this book. It would be possible to put this passage in the past and suppose it to have been spoken after Yen Hui's death; but I see no reason to do so.

2   i.e. whether he is fit to be entrusted with office. There is no need to have seen him actually handling practical issues. cf. *Mencius*, IV, A, 15.

3   Literally, 'warming up'. The business of the teacher is to give fresh life to the Scriptures by reinterpreting them so that they apply to the problems of modern life. All scriptures (Homer, the *Koran*, our own Bible) have been used in this way. I have seen 'The poor ye have always with you' used as an argument against slum-clearance. We have read above how Tzu-kung showed himself to be a true teacher by 'reanimating' a passage from the *Songs*.

4   i.e. a specialist, a tool used for a special purpose. He need only have general, moral qualifications.

15 The Master said, 'He who learns but does not think, is lost.' He who thinks but does not learn is in great danger.[1]

16 The Master said, He who sets to work upon a different strand destroys the whole fabric.[2]

17 The Master said, Yu,[3] shall I teach you what knowledge is? When you know a thing, to recognise that you know it, and when you do not know a thing, to recognise that you do not know it. That is knowledge.[4]

18 Tzu-chang was studying the *Song* Han-lu.[5] The Master said, Hear much, but maintain silence[6] as regards doubtful points and be cautious in speaking of the rest; then you will seldom get into trouble. See much, but ignore what it is dangerous to have seen, and be cautious in acting upon the rest; then you will seldom want to undo your acts. He who seldom gets into trouble about what he has said and seldom does anything that he afterwards wishes he had not done, will be sure incidentally[7] to get his reward.

1   I imagine that the first clause is a proverbial saying, and that Confucius meets it with the second clause. The proverb says: 'To learn without thinking is fatal.' Confucius says: To think but not to learn (i.e. study the Way of the ancients) is equally dangerous.

2   The metaphor is one of weaving or netting. 'Strand' (*tuan*) is a sprout, something that sticks out, and so 'the loose end of a thread'. The moral Way as opposed to the opportunist Way of the World must be followed consistently. It is no use working at it in disconnected patches.

3   Familiar name of the disciple Tzu-lu.

4   That knowledge consists in knowing that one does not know is a frequent theme in early Chinese texts. cf. *Tao Te Ching*, ch. 71.

5   *The Book of Songs*, p. 213. It puns on Han-lu, the name of a mountain, and *han-lu* 'seeking princely rewards, preferment.'

6   Literally, 'leave a gap', a metaphor derived from the language of copyists and scribes. cf. XV, 25.

7   See additional notes. From 'Hear much' to 'acts' is in rhyme, but would be awkward to print as verse.

19 Duke Ai[1] asked, What can I do in order to get the support of the common people? Master K'ung[2] replied, If you 'raise up the straight and set them on top of the crooked,' the commoners will support you. But if you raise the crooked and set them on top of the straight, the commoners will not support you.

20 Chi K'ang-tzu[3] asked whether there were any form of encouragement by which he could induce the common people to be respectful and loyal. The Master said, Approach them with dignity, and they will respect you. Show piety towards your parents and kindness towards your children, and they will be loyal to you. Promote those who are worthy, train those who are incompetent; that is the best form of encouragement.

21 Someone, when talking to Master K'ung, said, How is it that you are not in the public service? The Master said, The Book[4] says: 'Be filial, only be filial and friendly towards your brothers, and you will be contributing to government.' There are other sorts of service quite different from what you[5] mean by service.

22 The Master said, I do not see what use a man can be put to, whose word cannot be trusted. How can a waggon be made to go if it has no yoke-bar or a carriage, if it has no collar-bar?

1   Duke of Lu from 494–468 BC.
2   i.e. Confucius.
3   Head of the three families who were *de facto* rulers of Lu. Died 469 BC.
4   i.e. what Europeans call the *Book of History*. The passage does not occur in the genuine books. What it meant in its original context no doubt was 'Be pious to your ancestors . . . be generous in rewarding your officers of State.' Confucius 'reanimates' the ancient text, in order to prove that a virtuous private life makes a real contribution towards the public welfare.
5   *Ch'i* corresponds to the Latin *iste*.

23 Tzu-chang asked whether the state of things[1] ten generations hence could be foretold. The Master said, We know in what ways the Yin modified ritual when they followed upon the Hsia.[2] We know in what ways the Chou[3] modified ritual when they followed upon the Yin.[4] And hence we can foretell what the successors of Chou will be like, even supposing they do not appear till a hundred generations from now.

24 The Master said, Just as to sacrifice to ancestors other than one's own is presumption, so to see what is right and not do it is cowardice.

1 As regards ritual.
2 Supposed to have ruled in the 3rd and 2nd millennia BC.
3 The dynasty which still had a nominal hegemony in the time of Confucius.
4 The fall of Yin took place in the eleventh century BC. It was on the site of one of their capitals that the famous 'Honan oracle-bones' were found.

BOOK THREE

1 Master K'ung said of the head of the Chi family[1] when he had eight teams[2] of dancers performing in his courtyard, If this man can be endured, who cannot be endured!

2 The Three Families used the *Yung Song*[3] during the removal of the sacrificial vessels. The Master said,

> By rulers and lords attended,
> The Son of Heaven, mysterious —

What possible application can such words have in the hall of the Three Families?

3 The Master said, A man who is not Good, what can he have to do with ritual? A man who is not Good, what can he have to do with music?

4 Lin Fang asked for some main principles in connection with ritual. The Master said, A very big question. In ritual at large it is a safe rule always to be too sparing rather than too lavish; and in the particular case of mourning-rites, they should be dictated by grief rather than by fear.

1 One of the Three Families that had usurped most of the powers of the Duke of Lu.

2 See additional notes.

3 'He comes in solemn state . . .', *The Book of Songs*, p. 231. Its use was obviously only appropriate at the Emperor's Court. It would have been out of place at the Duke's palace, and was still more so in the hall of the Three Families.

5 The Master said, The barbarians of the East and North have retained their princes. They are not in such a state of decay as we in China.[1]

6 The head of the Chi family was going to make the offerings on Mount T'ai.[2] The Master said to Jan Ch'iu,[3] Cannot you save him from this? Jan Ch'iu replied, I cannot. The Master said, Alas, we can hardly suppose Mount T'ai to be ignorant of matters that even Lin Fang enquires into![4]

7 The Master said, Gentlemen never compete. You will say that in archery they do so. But even then they bow and make way for one another when they are going up to the archery-ground, when they are coming down and at the subsequent drinking-bout. Thus even when competing, they still remain gentlemen.

1 Where in several States the ruling families had been ousted by usurpers.
2 To the spirit of the mountain, a thing which the Duke alone had the right to do. The offering is said to have consisted of jade objects.
3 Who was in the service of the Chi family.
4 The mountain must surely know enough of ritual to be aware that no sacrifice but the Duke's could be accepted. The sense is carried on from IV, 4.

8   Tzu-hsia asked, saying, What is the meaning of

> Oh the sweet smile dimpling,
> The lovely eyes so black and white!
> Plain silk that you would take for coloured stuff.[1]

The Master said, The painting comes after the plain groundwork.[2] Tzu-hsia said, Then ritual comes afterwards?[3] The Master said, Shang[4] it is who bears me up. At last I have someone with whom I can discuss the Songs!

9   The Master said, How can we talk about the ritual of the Hsia? The State of Ch'i[5] supplies no adequate evidence. How can we talk about the ritual of Yin? The State of Sung supplies no adequate evidence. For there is a lack both of documents and of learned men. But for this lack we should be able to obtain evidence from these two States.

10   The Master said, At the Ancestral Sacrifice, as for all that comes after the libation, I had far rather not witness it![6]

---

1   So dazzling is the contrast that the effect is that of painted stuff rather than of a design in black and white. The first two lines occur in *Song* 86 where however they are not followed by the third line.

2   Confucius reinterprets the third line of verse in the sense 'It is on plain silk that one makes coloured designs', or the like. In scriptural reinterpretation the fact that the new meaning does not fit in with the original context is of no consequence.

3   Can only be built upon Goodness.

4   Familiar names of Tzu-hsia. For a further discussion of this passage, see additional notes.

5   In Honan, where descendants of the Hsia still carried on the sacrifices. Confucius laments that these States had not preserved the documents and rites of their ancestors. The interrogative particles seem to have been accidentally omitted.

6   In interpreting such passages as this we have to be careful not to read them in the light of later and to a large extent Utopian, theoretical books of ritual. Confucius was obviously displeased by the way in which the *Ti* (Ancestor-sacrifice) was carried out in Lu, presumably because it was too closely modelled on Imperial ritual; more than that we cannot say.

11 Someone asked for an explanation of the Ancestral Sacrifice. The Master said, I do not know. Anyone who knew the explanation could deal with all things under Heaven as easily as I lay this here; and he laid his finger upon the palm of his hand.[1]

12 Of the saying, 'The word "sacrifice" is like the word "present"; one should sacrifice to a spirit as though[2] that spirit was present', the Master said, If I am not present at the sacrifice, it is as though there were no sacrifice.[3]

13 Wang-sun Chia[4] asked about the meaning of the saying,

> Better pay court to the stove
> Than pay court to the Shrine.[5]

The Master said, It is not true. He who has put himself in the wrong with Heaven has no means of expiation left.

14 The Master said, Chou could survey the two preceding dynasties. How great a wealth of culture! And we follow upon Chou.[6]

1 For this anecdote, cf. *Chung Yung*, XIX, 6, and *K'ung Tzu Chia Yü*, 27, (Lun Li).

2 i.e. with the same demeanour and expression. cf. *Li Chi*, XIII, end, 'In general, in sacrifice demeanour and expression should be as though one were in the presence of the person who is being sacrificed to.'

3 i.e. do not worry about 'spirits being present' and the like. What matters is the state of mind of the sacrificer. If he is not heart and soul 'there', the sacrifice is useless. On the purely subjective value of sacrifice, see *Hsün Tzu*, P'ien XIX, end.

4 Commander-in-chief in the State of Wei, mentioned under the year 502 BC in the *Tso Chuan*.

5 This rhymed saying means that it is better to be on good terms with the hearth-god and have a full belly than waste one's food on the Ancestors, who cannot enjoy it. Confucius, who is usually able to reinterpret old maxims in a new, moral sense, finds himself obliged to reject this cynical piece of peasant-lore *in toto*.

6 i.e. we in Lu have all three dynasties, Hsia, Yin, and Chou to look back upon and imitate.

15 When the Master entered the Grand Temple[1] he asked questions about everything there. Someone said, Do not tell me that this son of a villager from Tsou[2] is expert in matters of ritual. When he went to the Grand Temple, he had to ask about everything. The Master hearing of this said, Just so! such is the ritual.[3]

16 The Master said, The saying

> In archery it is not the hide that counts,
> For some men have more strength than others,

is the way of the Ancients.[4]

17 Tzu-kung wanted to do away with the presentation[5] of a sacrificial sheep at the announcement[6] of each new moon. The Master said, Ssu! You grudge sheep, but I grudge ritual.

18 The Master said, Were anyone today to serve his prince according to the full prescriptions of ritual, he would be thought a sycophant.

19 Duke Ting (died 495 BC) asked for a precept concerning a ruler's use of his ministers and a minister's service to his ruler. Master K'ung replied saying, A ruler in employing his ministers should be guided solely by the prescriptions of ritual. Ministers in serving their ruler, solely by devotion to his cause.

1   Erected in honour of the first Duke of Chou.
2   A village with which Confucius's family had been connected.
3   i.e. precisely by doing so I showed my knowledge of ritual; for the asking of such questions is prescribed by ritual. For questions of this sort, see additional notes.
4   i.e. it is not piercing the hide stretched as a target that counts. In this ancient rhymed saying Confucius saw a maxim which metaphorically resumed the whole way of the Ancient Sages, who ruled by Goodness, not by force. For the first of the two lines, cf. *I Li*, Couvreur's translation, p. 173. cf. also *Chou Li*, where *chu p'i* seems merely to mean 'hitting the target'. See additional notes.
5   By the Duke to his State officers. This is the explanation of Liu T'ai-kung (1751–1805). See H.C.C.C. 798.
6   To the Ancestors, who are kept informed of everything that goes on below.

20 The Master said, The Ospreys![1] Pleasure not carried to the point of debauch; grief not carried to the point of self-injury.

21 Duke Ai asked Tsai Yü[2] about the Holy Ground. Tsai Yü replied, The Hsia sovereigns marked theirs with a pine, the men of Yin used a cypress, the men of Chou used a chestnut-tree, saying, 'This will cause the common people to be in fear and trembling.'[3] The Master hearing of it said, What is over and done with, one does not discuss. What has already taken its course, one does not criticise; what already belongs to the past, one does not censure.[4]

22 The Master said, Kuan Chung[5] was in reality a man of very narrow capacities. Someone said, Surely he displayed an example of frugality? The Master said, Kuan had three lots of wives,[6] his State officers performed no double duties. How can he be cited as an example of frugality? That may be, the other said; but surely he had a great knowledge of ritual? The Master said, Only the ruler of a State may build a screen to mask his gate; but Kuan had such

---

1 *The Book of Songs*, No. 87, which begins by describing a lover's grief at being separated from his lady and ends by describing their joyful union. Confucius sees in it a general guide to conduct, whether in joy or affliction. The opening words are: 'Kuan, kuan cry the ospreys.'

2 A disciple in whom Confucius was much disappointed.

3 Pun on *li* a chestnut-tree and *li* 'to be in awe'.

4 The usual explanation of this passage makes Confucius's comment refer to Tsai Yü's pun 'which might lead the Duke to severe measures' in dealing with his people (Legge, p. 26). The comment, however, is phrased in such a way that it must be taken as referring to the remote and not to the immediate past. It is perhaps unfortunate, Confucius suggests, that the founders of the Chou dynasty chose a tree with so inauspicious a name; but it was ill-bred of Tsai Yü to criticise them in conversation with Duke Ai of Lu, who was their direct descendant.

5 Kuan Tzu, seventh century BC, the statesman who built up the power of the Ch'i kingdom. Confucius regarded him as having merely increased the political prestige of his country without raising its moral status.

6 Each consisting of a wife and two 'understudies' (bridesmaids); only a feudal lord was entitled to such an establishment.

a screen. Only the ruler of a State, when meeting another such ruler, may use cup-mounds;[1] but Kuan used one. If even Kuan is to be cited as an expert in ritual, who is not an expert in ritual?

23   When talking to the Grand Master[2] of Lu about music, the Master said, Their music[3] in so far as one can find out about it began with a strict unison. Soon the musicians were given more liberty;[4] but the tone remained harmonious, brilliant, consistent, right on till the close.

24   The guardian of the frontier-mound at I[5] asked to be presented to the Master, saying, No gentleman arriving at this frontier has ever yet failed to accord me an interview. The Master's followers presented him. On going out the man said, Sirs, you must not be disheartened by his failure. It is now a very long while[6] since the Way prevailed in the world. I feel sure that Heaven intends to use your Master as a wooden bell.[7]

25   The Master spoke of the Succession Dance[8] as being[9] perfect beauty and at the same time perfect goodness; but of the War Dance as being perfect beauty, but not perfect goodness.

26   The Master said, High office filled by men of narrow views, ritual performed without reverence, the forms of mourning observed without grief — these are things I cannot bear to see!

1   A mound upon which to stand pledge-cups.
2   The *maestro*, music-master, who was always a blind man.
3   The music of the ancients.
4   To improvise.
5   On the borders of the State of Wei.
6   Sages appear at regular intervals. One is now due.
7   A rattle, used to arouse the populace in times of night-danger, and in general by heralds and town-criers; cf. *Li Chi*, Yüeh-ling. (Couvreur's translation, 1, 343).
8   This dance (at any rate according to the later Confucian theory) mimed the peaceful accession of the legendary Emperor Shun; the War Dance mimed the accession by conquest of the Emperor Wu, who overthrew the Yin. See above, II, 23.
9   Or as we should say, 'as embodying'.

BOOK FOUR

1   The Master said, It is Goodness that gives to a neighbourhood its beauty.[1] One who is free to choose, yet does not prefer to dwell among the Good – how can he be accorded the name of wise?[2]

2   The Master said, Without Goodness a man

> Cannot for long endure adversity,
> Cannot for long enjoy prosperity.

The Good Man rests content with Goodness; he that is merely wise pursues Goodness in the belief that it pays to do so.

3, 4   Of the adage[3] 'Only a Good Man knows how to like people, knows how to dislike them,' the Master said, He whose heart is in the smallest degree set upon Goodness will dislike no one.

---

1   cf. *Mencius*, II, A, 7.

2   A justification of the maxim, 'When right does not prevail in a kingdom, then leave it,' and of Confucius's own prolonged travels.

3   cf. *Ta Hsüeh* (The Great Learning), commentary, X, 15. 'Only the Good man is considered capable of loving (*ai*) men, capable of hating them.' In the *Kuo Yü* (ch. 18), however, the saying is quite differently interpreted: 'Only a good man is safe to like and safe to dislike . . . For if you like him, he will not take undue advantage of it; and if you dislike him, he will not resent it.' The words 'The Master said' at the beginning of paragraph 3 should be omitted, and paragraphs 3 and 4 taken together.

5   Wealth and rank are what every man desires; but if they can only be retained to the detriment of the Way he professes, he must relinquish them. Poverty and obscurity are what every man detests; but if they can only be avoided to the detriment of the Way he professes, he must accept them. The gentleman who ever parts company with Goodness does not fulfil that name. Never for a moment[1] does a gentleman quit the way of Goodness. He is never so harried but that he cleaves to this; never so tottering but that he cleaves to this.

6   The Master said, I for my part[2] have never yet seen one who really cared for Goodness, nor one who really abhorred wickedness. One who really cared for Goodness would never let any other consideration come first. One who abhorred wickedness would be so constantly doing Good that wickedness would never have a chance to get at him. Has anyone ever managed to do Good with his whole might even as long as the space of a single day? I think not. Yet I for my part have never seen anyone give up such an attempt because he had not the *strength* to go on. It may well have happened, but I for my part have never seen it.[3]

7   The Master said, Every man's faults belong to a set.[4] If one looks out for faults it is only as a means of recognising Goodness.

8   The Master said, In the morning, hear the Way; in the evening, die content![5]

9   The Master said, A Knight whose heart is set upon the Way, but who is ashamed of wearing shabby clothes and eating coarse food, is not worth calling into counsel.

1   Literally, 'for as long as it takes to eat' one bowl of rice. A common impression, simply meaning a very little while.
2   *Wo* as a nominative is more emphatic than *wu*.
3   It is the will not the way that is wanting.
4   i.e. a set of qualities which includes virtues.
5   The well-known saying *Vedi Napoli e poi mori* [See Naples and then die] follows the same pattern. The meaning is, you will have missed nothing.

10 The Master said, A gentleman in his dealings with the world has neither enmities nor affections;[1] but wherever he sees Right he ranges himself beside it.

11 The Master said, Where gentlemen set their hearts upon moral force (*te*)[2] the commoners set theirs upon the soil.[3] Where gentlemen think only of punishments, the commoners think only of exemptions.[4]

12 The Master said, Those[5] whose measures are dictated by mere expediency will arouse continual discontent.

13 The Master said, If it is really possible to govern countries by ritual and yielding, there is no more to be said. But if it is not really possible, of what use is ritual?[6]

14 The Master said, He[7] does not mind not being in office; all he minds about is whether he has qualities that entitle him to office. He does not mind failing to get recognition; he is too busy doing the things that entitle him to recognition.

1 Reading uncertain, but general sense quite clear.
2 As opposed to physical compulsion. See additional notes.
3 They *an t'u*, 'are content with the soil', and are prepared to defend it.
4 *Hui* means amnesties, immunities, exemptions, as opposed to what is 'lawful and proper'.
5 The rulers and upper classes in general.
6 The saying can be paraphrased as follows: If I and my followers are right in saying that countries can be governed solely by correct carrying out of ritual and its basic principle of 'giving way to others', there is obviously no case to be made out for any other form of government. If on the other hand we are wrong, then ritual is useless. To say, as people often do, that ritual is all very well so long as it is not used as an instrument of government, is wholly to misunderstand the purpose of ritual.
7 The gentleman. But we might translate 'I do not mind', etc.

15   The Master said, Shên! My Way has one (thread) that runs right
     through it. Master Tsêng said, Yes. When the Master had gone
     out, the disciples asked, saying What did he mean? Master Tsêng
     said, Our Master's Way is simply this: Loyalty, consideration.[1]

16   The Master said, A gentleman takes as much trouble to discover
     what is right as lesser men take to discover what will pay.

17   The Master said, In the presence of a good man, think all the
     time how you may learn to equal him. In the presence of a bad
     man, turn your gaze within![2]

18   The Master said, In serving his father and mother a man may
     gently remonstrate with them. But if he sees that he has failed to
     change their opinion, he should resume an attitude of deference
     and not thwart them; may feel discouraged, but not resentful.

19   The Master said, While father and mother are alive, a good son
     does not wander far afield; or if he does so, goes only where he
     has said he was going.[3]

20   The Master said, If for the whole three years of mourning a son
     manages to carry on the household exactly as in his father's day,
     then he is a good son indeed.[4]

21   The Master said, It is always better for a man to know the age of
     his parents. In the one case[5] such knowledge will be a comfort to
     him; in the other,[6] it will fill him with a salutary dread.

1   Loyalty to superiors; consideration for the feelings of others, 'not doing
     to them anything one would not like to have done to oneself', as
     defined below, XV, 23. 'Loyalty and Consideration' is one of the Nine
     Virtues enumerated by the *I Chou Shu*, 29, I verso. cf. also XV, 2 below.
2   'Within yourself scrutinise yourself'. *êrh* is the second person singular
     pronoun, not the conjunction?
3   Particularly in order that if they die he may be able to come back and
     perform the rites of mourning.
4   cf. I, 11.
5   If he knows that they are not so old as one might think.
6   If he realises that they are very old.

22 The Master said, In old days a man kept a hold on his words, fearing the disgrace that would ensue should he himself fail to keep pace with them.

23 The Master said, Those who err on the side of strictness are few indeed!

24 The Master said, A gentleman covets the reputation of being slow in word but prompt in deed.[1]

25 The Master said, Moral force (*te*) never dwells in solitude; it will always bring neighbours.[2]

26 Tzu-yu said, In the service of one's prince repeated scolding[3] can only lead to loss of favour; in friendship, it can only lead to estrangement.

---

1   cf. *Tao Te Ching*, ch. 45
2   Whenever one individual or one country substitutes *te* for physical compulsion, other individuals or other countries inevitably follow suit.
3   cf. XII, 23 and additional notes.

BOOK FIVE

1   The Master said of Kung Yeh Ch'ang, Though he has suffered imprisonment, he is not an unfit person to choose as a husband; for it was not through any fault of his own. He married him to his daughter.

   The Master said of Nan Jung,[1] In a country ruled according to the Way, he would not be overlooked; in a country not ruled according to the Way, he would manage to avoid capital punishment or mutilation. He married him to his elder brother's[2] daughter.

2   Of Tzu-chien[3] he said, A gentleman indeed is such a one as he! If the land of Lu were indeed without gentlemen, how could he have learnt this?

3   Tzu-kung asked saying, What do you think of me? The Master said, You are a vessel.[4] Tzu-kung said, What sort of vessel? The Master said, A sacrificial vase of jade![5]

1   The commentators identify Nan Jung with Nan-kung Kuo, son of Mêng I Tzu, head of the powerful Mêng Family. This is, however, no ground for this identification, nor any reason to suppose that Confucius ever formed so exalted a family connection.

2   According to later tradition Confucius's elder brother was a cripple and for this reason his duties devolved on Confucius.

3   The disciple Fu Tzu-chien, who figures in later legend as model governor of the town of Shan-fu. See additional notes.

4   A man of particular capacities, but lacking the general state of electness known as *Jen* (Goodness).

5   i.e. the highest sort of vessel.

4   Someone said, Jan Yung is Good, but he is a poor talker. The Master said, What need has he to be a good talker? Those who down others with clap-trap are seldom popular. Whether he is Good, I do not know. But I see no need for him to be a good talker.

5   The Master gave Ch'i-tiao K'ai leave to take office, but he replied, 'I have not yet sufficiently perfected myself in the virtue of good faith.' The Master was delighted.

6   The Master said, The Way makes no progress. I shall get upon a raft and float out to sea.[1] I am sure Yu would come with me. Tzu-lu on hearing of this was in high spirits. The Master said, That is Yu indeed! He sets far too much store by feats of physical daring. It seems as though I should never get hold of the right sort of people.[2]

7   Mêng Wu Po[3] asked whether Tzu-lu was Good. The Master said, I do not know. On his repeating the question the Master said, In a country of a thousand war-chariots Yu could be trusted to carry out the recruiting. But whether he is Good I do not know. 'What about Ch'iu?'[4] The Master said, In a city of a thousand families or a baronial family with a hundred chariots he might do well as Warden. But whether he is Good, I do not know. 'What about Ch'ih?'[5] The Master said, Girt with his sash, standing in his place

---

1   What Confucius proposes is, of course, to go and settle among the barbarians. cf. III, 5 and IX, 13. A certain idealisation of the 'noble savage' is to be found fairly often in early Chinese literature; cf. the eulogy of the barbarians put into the mouth of a Chinese whose ancestors had settled among them, *Shih Chi* V, and the maxim 'When the Emperor no longer functions, learning must be sought among the Four Barbarians', north, west, east, and south (*Tso Chuan*, Chao kung seventeenth year).

2   Literally, 'get material'. cf. *I Chou Shu* VIII, I verso. Yu (familiar name of Tzu-lu) figures in later legend as a converted swashbuckler, who constantly shocked Confucius by his pugnacity.

3   See above, II, 6.

4   The disciple Jan Ch'iu.

5   The disciple Kung-hsi Hua.

at Court he might well be charged to converse with strangers and guests. But whether he is Good, I do not know.[1]

8   The Master in discussing Tzu-kung said to him, Which do you yourself think is the better, you or Hui?[2] He answered saying, I dare not so much as look at Hui. For Hui has but to hear one part in ten, in order to understand the whole ten. Whereas if I hear one part, I understand no more than two parts. The Master said, Not equal to him – you and I are not equal to him!

9   Tsai Yü[3] used to sleep during the day. The Master said, Rotten wood cannot be carved, nor a wall of dried dung be trowelled.[4] What use is there in my scolding him any more?

     The Master said, There was a time when I merely listened attentively to what people said, and took for granted that they would carry out their words. Now I am obliged not only to give ear to what they say, but also to keep an eye on what they do. It was my dealings with Tsai Yü that brought about the change.

10   The Master said, I have never yet seen a man who was truly steadfast.[5] Someone answered saying, 'Shên Ch'êng'. The Master said, Ch'êng! He is at the mercy of his desires. How can *he* be called steadfast?

11   Tzu-kung said, What I do not want others to do to me, I have no desire to do to others. The Master said, Oh Ssu! You have not quite got to that point yet.

1   Jan Ch'iu is known to history as a faithful henchman of the Lu dictator. Kung-hsi Hua's ambition was to perfect himself in the etiquette of State ceremonies. See XI, 25.

2   See above, II, 9.

3   See III, 21.

4   i.e. patterned with the trowel. To translate 'be plastered' destroys the parallelism.

5   Impervious to outside influences, intimidations, etc.

12 Tzu-kung said, Our Master's views concerning culture and the outward insignia[1] of goodness, we are permitted to hear; but about Man's nature[2] and the ways of Heaven[3] he will not tell us anything at all.

13 When Tzu-lu heard any precept and was still trying unsuccessfully to put it into practice, his one fear was that he might hear some fresh precept.

14 Tzu-kung asked saying, Why was K'ung Wên Tzu called Wên (The Cultured)?[4] The Master said, Because he was diligent[5] and so fond of learning that he was not ashamed to pick up knowledge even from his inferiors.

15 Of Tzu-ch'an[6] the Master said that in him were to be found four of the virtues that belong to the Way of the true gentleman. In his private conduct he was courteous, in serving his master he was punctilious, in providing for the needs of the people he gave them even more than their due; in exacting service from the people, he was just.

1 *Chang* (insignia) means literally 'emblems' (usually representations of birds, beasts or plants) figuring on banners or dresses to show the rank of the owner. Hence metaphorically, the outward manifestations of an inner virtue.

2 As it is before it has been embellished with 'culture'.

3 T'ien Tao. The Tao taught by Confucius only concerned human behaviour (the ways of man); he did not expound a corresponding Heavenly Tao, governing the conduct of unseen powers and divinities.

4 i.e. why was he accorded this posthumous title? He was a statesman of the Wei State who died between 484 and 480 BC. He figures in the chronicles as a disloyal and self-seeking minister.

5 There is perhaps a play on *wên* and *min* (diligent); the two words were pronounced very similarly in ancient Chinese.

6 Minister in the Chêng State; died 522 BC.

16 The Master said, Yen P'ing Chung is[1] a good example of what one's intercourse with one's fellow men should be. However long he has known anyone he always maintains the same scrupulous courtesy.

17 The Master said, Tsang Wên Chung[2] kept a Ts'ai tortoise[3] in a hall with the hill-pattern on its pillar tops and the duckweed pattern on its king-posts.[4] Of what sort, pray, was his knowledge?[5]

18 Tzu-chang asked saying, The Grand Minister Tzu-wên[6] was appointed to this office on three separate occasions, but did not on any of these three occasions display the least sign of elation. Three times he was deposed; but never showed the least sign of disappointment. Each time, he duly informed his successor concerning the administration of State affairs during his tenure of office. What should you say of him? The Master said, He was certainly faithful to his prince's interests. Tzu-chang said, Would you not call him Good? The Master said, I am not sure. I see nothing in that to merit the title Good.

    (Tzu-chang said) When Ts'ui Tzu assassinated the sovereign of Ch'i,[7] Ch'ên Wên Tzu[8] who held a fief of ten war chariots gave it up and went away. On arriving in another State, he said, 'I can see they are no better here than our minister Ts'ui Tzu'; and he

---

1   Or 'was'. The Ch'i minister Yen Tzu, famous for his wise counsels, died in 500 BC.

2   Minister of Lu in the seventh century BC.

3   The country of Ts'ai was famous for its tortoises.

4   Such decoration was proper only to the Emperor's ancestral temple and palace. cf. *I Chou Shu* 48, end. Kuan Tzu (*Li Chi*, Tsa Ch'i, Couvreur's translation, II, 187) is accused of decorating his palace in the same way.

5   i.e. his knowledge of ritual. For a tortoise kept on a special terrace and smeared daily with the blood of four bulls, see *Kuan Tzu*, P'ien 75. Strictly speaking only rulers kept tortoises for use in divination *(Li Chi* X); ministers used the yarrow-stalks. But we find Tsang's grandson still in possession of a Ts'ai tortoise (*Tso Chuan*, Duke Hsiang twenty-third year); so perhaps the family claimed an hereditary privilege.

6   Middle of the seventh century BC.

7   In 548 BC the Duke of Ch'i had seduced his wife.

8   Another Ch'i minister.

went away. On arriving in the next country, he said, 'I can see they are no better here than our minister Ts'ui Tzu'; and went away. What should you say of him? The Master said, He was certainly scrupulous. Tzu-chang said, Would you not call him Good? The Master said, I am not sure. I see nothing in that to merit the title Good.

19 Chi Wên Tzu[1] used to think thrice before acting. The Master hearing of it said, Twice is quite enough.[2]

20 The Master said, Ning Wu Tzu[3] 'so long as the Way prevailed in his country he showed wisdom; but when the Way no longer prevailed, he showed his folly.'[4] To such wisdom as his we may all attain; but not to such folly!

21 When the Master was in Ch'ên[5] he said, Let us go back, let us go back! The little ones[6] at home are headstrong and careless. They are perfecting themselves in all the showy insignia of culture without any idea how to use them.

22 The Master said, Po I and Shu Ch'i[7] never bore old ills in mind and had but the faintest feelings of rancour.

1 Died 568 BC.
2 Ch'êng Hao (AD 1032-1085) says that if one thinks more than twice, self-interest begins to come into play.
3 A minister of Wei (seventh century BC), famous for his blind devotion to his prince, whose enemies had incarcerated him in a deep dungeon. Here Ning managed to feed his prince through a tube.
4 Such was the judgment of the world.
5 About 492 BC?
6 Disciples.
7 Legendary brothers, almost always bracketed together in this way. The 'old ills' were the misdeeds of the last Yin ruler. When he was attacked by the Chou tribe, the brothers refused to take up arms against their sovereign, despite his great wickedness. Their lack of yüan (rancour) was a classical theme; cf. VII, 14. This was shown by their attitude after each in turn had resigned his rights of accession to the rulership of the small State to which they belonged. Having proposed this act of 'cession' (jang), they carried it out loyally and uncomplainingly.

23 The Master said, How can we call even Wei-shêng Kao upright?
    When someone asked him for vinegar he went and begged it
    from the people next door, and then gave it as though it were his
    own gift.[1]

24 The Master said, Clever talk, a pretentious manner and a
    reverence that is only of the feet[2] – Tso Ch'iu Ming[3] was
    incapable of stooping to them, and I too could never stoop to
    them. Having to conceal one's indignation and keep on friendly
    terms with the people against whom one feels it – Tso Ch'iu
    Ming was incapable of stooping to such conduct, and I too am
    incapable of stooping to such conduct.[4]

25 Once when Yen Hui and Tzu-lu were waiting upon him the
    Master said, Suppose each of you were to tell his wish. Tzu-lu said,
    I should like to have carriages and horses, clothes and fur rugs,
    share them with my friends and feel no annoyance if they were
    returned to me the worse for wear. Yen Hui said, I should like
    never to boast of my good qualities nor make a fuss about the
    trouble I take on behalf of others. Tzu-lu said, A thing I should like

---

1   Wei-shêng Kao (see *Chuang Tzu* XXIX, I, *Chan Kuo Ts'ê*, Yen
    stories, Pt. 1, *Huai-nan Tzu* XVII, end) is the legendary paragon of
    truthfulness. Confucius adopts the same formula as the rhyme:

>   The Germans in Greek
>   Are sadly to seek.
>   All except Hermann;
>   And Hermann is a German.

    How rare, how almost non-existent a quality uprightness must be,
    Confucius bitterly says, if even into the legend of the most upright of
    all men there has crept an instance of falsity!
    Translators have supposed Wei-shêng Kao to have been some actual
    contemporary of Confucius, whose conduct the Master was criticising.
    This misses the whole point.
2   cf. *Ta Tai Li Chi*, 49, where 'foot reverence' is coupled with 'mouth
    holiness'.
3   See additional notes.
4   And am therefore unfitted for court life, where such behaviour is the
    sole way to preferment.

is to hear the Master's wish. The Master said, In dealing with the aged, to be of comfort to them; in dealing with friends, to be of good faith with them; in dealing with the young, to cherish them.

26 The Master said, In vain have I looked for a single man capable of seeing his own faults and bringing the charge home against himself.

27 The Master said, In an hamlet of ten houses you may be sure of finding someone quite as loyal and true to his word as I. But I doubt if you would find anyone with such a love of learning.[1]

1   i.e. self-improvement in the most general sense. Not book-learning.

BOOK SIX

1   The Master said, Now Yung,[1] for example. I should not mind
    setting him with his face to the south.[2] Jan Yung then asked
    about Tzu-sang Po-tzu.[3] The Master said, He too would do. He
    is lax.[4] Jan Yung said, I can understand that such a man might do
    as a ruler, provided he were scrupulous in his own conduct and
    lax only in his dealings[5] with the people. But you would admit
    that a man who was lax in his own conduct as well as in
    government would be too lax.[6] The Master said, What Yung
    says is quite true.

2   Duke Ai asked which of the disciples had a love of learning.
    Master K'ung answered him saying, There was Yen Hui. He had
    a great love of learning. He never vented his wrath upon the
    innocent nor let others suffer for his faults. Unfortunately the
    span of life allotted to him by Heaven was short, and he died. At
    present there are none or at any rate I have heard of none who
    are fond of learning.[7]

1   The disciple Jan Yung.
2   Trying him as a ruler.
3   cf. the Tzu-sang of *Chuang Tzu* VI, 11.
4   This is a paradox, *chien* (lax) being generally used in a bad sense.
5   i.e. in the exaction of taxes, corvées, and the like. I punctuate after
    ching, not after *chien*.
6   i.e. too lax to 'set with his face to the south'.
7   cf. XI, 6.

3   When Kung-hsi Hua was sent on a mission to Ch'i, Master Jan asked[1] that Hua's mother might be granted an allowance of grain. The Master said, Give her a cauldron[2] full. Jan said that was not enough. The Master said, Give her a measure.[3] Master Jan gave her five bundles.[4] The Master said, When Ch'ih[5] went to Ch'i he drove sleek horses and was wrapped in light furs. There is a saying, A gentleman helps out the necessitous; he does not make the rich richer still.

When Yüan Ssu was made a governor, he was given an allowance of nine hundred measures of grain, but declined it. The Master said, Surely you could find people who would be glad of it among your neighbours or in your village?

4   The Master said of Jan Yung, If the offspring of a brindled[6] ox is ruddy-coated[7] and has grown its horns, however much people might hesitate to use it,[8] would the hills and streams really reject it?

5   The Master said, Hui is[9] capable of occupying his whole mind for three months on end with no thought but that of Goodness. The others can do so, some for a day, some even for a month; but that is all.[10]

1   i.e. asked the government (the Chi Family), in whose service he was.

2   A merely nominal amount. Confucius disapproved of her being given any at all.

3   A good deal more; but still not a great deal.

4   Ten times (?) more than a measure. Jan entirely disregards Confucius's advice.

5   i.e. Kung-hsi Hua. He ought to have left behind sufficient provision for his mother.

6   i.e. one unsuitable for sacrifice.

7   All over. Only animals of one colour could be used for sacrifice.

8   In sacrificing to the hills and streams. The implication is that Jan Yung was of humble origin. This, says Confucius, ought not to prejudice us against him.

9   There is nothing to indicate whether this was said before or after Yen Hui's premature death.

10   On the strength of sayings such as this, the Taoists claimed Yen Hui as an exponent of *tso-wang* (sitting with blank mind), the Chinese equivalent of yoga.

6 Chi K'ang-tzu[1] asked whether Tzu-lu was the right sort of person to put into office. The Master said, Yu is efficient. It goes without saying that he is capable of holding office. Chi K'ang-tzu said, How about Tzu-kung? Would he be the right sort of person to put into office? The Master said, He can turn his merits to account.[2] It goes without saying, that he is capable of holding office. Chi K'ang-tzu said, How about Jan Ch'iu? Would he be the right sort of person to put into office? The Master said, He is versatile. It goes without saying that he is capable of holding office.

7 The Chi Family[3] wanted to make Min Tzu-ch'ien governor of Pi.[4] Min Tzu-ch'ien said, Invent a polite excuse for me. If that is not accepted and they try to get at me again, I shall certainly install myself on the far side of the Wên.[5]

8 When Jan Kêng was ill, the Master went to enquire after him, and grasping his hand through the window said, It is all over with him! Heaven has so ordained it – [6] But that such a man should have such an illness! That such a man should have such an illness![7]

9 The Master said, Incomparable indeed was Hui! A handful[8] of rice to eat, a gourdful of water to drink, living in a mean street – others would have found it unendurably depressing, but to Hui's cheerfulness it made no difference at all. Incomparable indeed was Hui![9]

1 Became head of the actual administration of Lu in 492 BC.
2 For *ta*, see additional notes.
3 i.e. the government. He would not serve a usurper.
4 The great stronghold of the Chi Family.
5 i.e. I shall take refuge in the neighbouring land of Ch'i, where I cannot be got at. He was faithful to the legitimate ruler, the Duke of Lu.
6 And we must not repine.
7 Later tradition very naturally explains the passage by saying that Jan Kêng's illness was leprosy. This fits in with the concluding words and also explains why Confucius did not enter the house.
8 Literally, a split bamboo-sectionful.
9 cf. *Mencius*, IV, B, 29.

10 Jan Ch'iu said, It is not that your Way does not commend itself to me, but that it demands powers I do not possess. The Master said, He whose strength gives out collapses during the course of the journey (the Way); but you deliberately draw the line.[1]

11 The Master said to Tzu-hsia, You must practise the *ju*[2] of gentlemen, not that of the common people.

12 When Tzu-yu was Warden of the castle of Wu, the Master said, Have you managed to get hold of the right sort of people there? Tzu-yu said, There is someone called T'an-t'ai Mieh-ming who 'walks on no bypaths'.[3] He has not once come to my house except on public business.

13 The Master said, Mêng Chih-fan is no boaster. When his people were routed[4] he was the last to flee; but when they neared the city-gate, he whipped up his horses, saying, It was not courage that kept me behind. My horses were slow.

14 The Master said, Without the eloquence of the priest[5] T'o and the beauty of Prince Ch'ao of Sung it is hard nowadays to get through.

1 Metaphor of marking boundary-lines of estates or the like.
2 A word of very uncertain meaning. Perhaps 'unwarlikeness'. See additional notes. The meaning of the saying may be 'The unwarlikeness of gentlemen means a preference for *te* (moral force), that of inferior people is mere cowardice.'
  Hu came ultimately to be the general name for followers of the Confucian Way.
3 i.e. strictly follows our Way. There is probably some further point in this story that is lost to us owing to our knowing so little about T'an-t'ai Mieh-ming.
4 At a battle with Ch'i outside the Lu capital in 484 BC. To belittle his own achievements (the opposite of boasting) is the duty of a gallant gentleman. So a modern airman who had stayed behind to fight a rear action might say, 'I was in a funk all the time, but I couldn't get away; my engine was missing fire.'
5 The *chu* (priest) recited invocations addressed to the ancestors. Both T'o and Chao flourished about 500 BC.

15 The Master said, Who expects to be able to go out of a house except by the door? How is it then that no one follows this Way of ours?[1]

16 The Master said, When natural substance prevails over ornamentation,[2] you get the boorishness of the rustic. When ornamentation prevails over natural substance, you get the pedantry of the scribe. Only when ornament and substance are duly blended do you get the true gentleman.

17 The Master said, Man's very life is honesty, in that without it he will be lucky indeed if he escapes with his life.[3]

18 The Master said, To prefer it[4] is better than only to know it. To delight in it is better than merely to prefer it.

19 The Master said, To men who have risen at all above the middling sort, one may talk of things higher yet. But to men who are at all below the middling sort it is useless to talk of things that are above them.[5]

20 Fan Ch'ih asked about wisdom.[6] The Master said, He who devotes himself to securing for his subjects what it is right they should have, who by respect for the Spirits keeps them at a distance,[7] may be termed wise. He asked about Goodness. The Master said, Goodness cannot be obtained till what is difficult[8] has been duly done. He who has done this may be called Good.

1 Though it is the obvious and only legitimate way out of all our difficulties.
2 i.e. when nature prevails over culture.
3 I punctuate after *chih*, not after *yeh*.
4 The Way.
5 That belong to a higher stage of learning.
6 i.e. to what rulers the title 'Wise' could be accorded.
7 When the Spirits of hills and streams do not receive their proper share of ritual and sacrifice they do not 'keep their distance', but 'possess' human beings, causing madness, sickness, pestilence, etc.
8 This only becomes intelligible when we refer to XIV, 2, where we see that the 'difficult thing' is to rid oneself of love of mastery, vanity, resentment, and covetousness.

21 The Master said, The wise man delights in water, the Good man delights in mountains. For the wise move; but the Good stay still. The wise are happy; but the Good, secure.[1]

22 A single change could bring Ch'i to the level of Lu; and a single change would bring Lu to the Way.

23 The Master said, A horn-gourd that is neither horn nor gourd! A pretty horn-gourd indeed, a pretty horn-gourd indeed.[2]

24 Tsai Yü asked saying, I take it a Good Man, even if he were told that another Good Man were at the bottom of a well, would go to join him? The Master said, Why should you think so? 'A gentleman can be broken, but cannot be dented;[3] may be deceived, but cannot be led astray.'[4]

24 (Paraphrased). Tsai Yü half playfully asked whether, since the Good always go to where other Good Men are, a Good Man would leap into a well on hearing that there was another Good Man at the bottom of it. Confucius, responding in the same playful spirit, quotes a maxim about the true gentleman, solely for the sake of the reference in it to *hsien,* which means 'throw down' into a pit or well, but also has the sense 'to pit', 'to dent'.

25 The Master said, A gentleman who is widely versed in letters and at the same time knows how to submit his learning to the restraints of ritual is not likely, I think, to go far wrong.

1 For the origin of this saying, which has here taken on a form distorted by quietist influences, see additional note.

2 A particular sort of bronze goblet was called *ku,* which is written 'horn' beside 'gourd', though the object in question is not shaped like a gourd and is not a drinking-horn. The saying is, of course, a metaphorical way of lamenting over the political state of China, 'ruled over' by an Emperor who had no temporal power and local sovereigns whose rights had been usurped by their ministers.

3 cf. *Shuo Yüan,* XVII: The gentleman (like jade) can be broken, but not bent.

4 i.e. deceived as to facts; but cannot be enticed into wrong conduct. cf. *Mencius,* V, A, 2

26 When the Master went to see Nan-tzu,[1] Tzu-lu was not pleased. Whereupon the Master made a solemn declaration[2] concerning his visit, saying, Whatsoever I have done amiss, may Heaven avert it, may Heaven avert it!

27 The Master said, How transcendent is the moral power of the Middle Use![3] That it is but rarely found among the common people is a fact long admitted.[4]

28 Tzu-kung said, If a ruler not only conferred wide benefits upon the common people, but also compassed the salvation of the whole State, what would you say of him? Surely, you would call him Good? The Master said, It would no longer be a matter of 'Good'. He would without doubt be a Divine Sage. Even Yao and Shun could hardly criticise him.[5] As for Goodness – you yourself desire rank and standing; then help others to get rank and standing. You want to turn your own merits to account; then help others to turn theirs to account – in fact, the ability to take one's own feelings as a guide – that is the sort of thing that lies in the direction of Goodness.[6]

1 The wicked concubine of Duke Ling of Wei.
2 See additional notes.
3 Confucius's Way was essentially one of moderation: 'to exceed is as bad as to fall short'. See additional notes.
4 *Chiu i* constantly has an idiomatic sense of this sort, and does not mean simply 'a long while'. cf. *Doctrine of the Mean,* III.
5 cf. XIV, 45, and *Han Shih Wai Chuan,* VII, 9.
6 For *fang,* 'direction', cf. XI, 25.

BOOK SEVEN

I, 2, 3 The Master said, I have 'transmitted what was taught to me without making up anything of my own'.[1] I have been faithful to and loved the Ancients. In these respects, I make bold to think, not even our old P'êng[2] can have excelled me. The Master said, I have listened in silence and noted what was said, I have never grown tired of learning nor wearied of teaching others what I have learnt. These at least are merits which I can confidently claim.[3] The Master said, The thought that 'I have left my moral power (te) untended, my learning unperfected, that I have heard of righteous men, but been unable to go to them; have heard of evil men, but been unable to reform them'[4] – it is these thoughts that disquiet me

4 In his leisure hours the Master's manner was very free-and-easy, and his expression alert and cheerful.

5 The Master said, How utterly have things gone to the bad with me! It is long now indeed since I dreamed that I saw the Duke of Chou.

1 cf. *Mo Tzu*, P'ien 46. 'A gentleman does not make anything up; he merely transmits.'
2 The Chinese Nestor. It is the special business of old men to transmit traditions.
3 For the idiom *ho yu*, 'there is no further trouble about', see above, IV, 13.
4 The passage in inverted commas consists of two rhymed couplets, and is probably traditional.

6   The Master said, Set your heart upon the Way, support yourself by its power, lean upon Goodness, seek distraction in the arts.[1]

7   The Master said, From the very poorest upwards – beginning even with the man who could bring no better present than a bundle of dried flesh[2] – none has ever come to me without receiving instruction.

8   The Master said, Only one who bursts with eagerness do I instruct; only one who bubbles with excitement, do I enlighten. If I hold up one corner and a man cannot come back to me with the other three,[3] I do not continue the lesson.

9   If at a meal the Master found himself seated next to someone who was in mourning, he did not eat his fill. When he had wailed at a funeral, during the rest of the day he did not sing.[4]

10 The Master said to Yen Hui, The maxim

When wanted, then go;
When set aside; then hide.

is one that you and I could certainly fulfil. Tzu-lu said, Supposing you had command of the Three Hosts,[5] whom would you take to help you? The Master said, The man who was ready to 'beard a tiger or rush a river'[6] without caring whether he lived or died – that sort of man I should not take. I should certainly take someone who approached difficulties with due caution and who preferred to succeed by strategy.

---

1   Music, archery and the like.
2   See additional notes.
3   Metaphor from laying out of field-plots?
4   Both of these are common ritual prescriptions. cf. *Li Chi* III, fol. 6 and I, fol. 6.
5   i.e. the whole army.
6   cf. *The Book of Songs*, No. 295, verse 6. The reply is clearly intended as a snub to the impulsive Tzu-lu. The song is one which I omit in my translation.

11 The Master said, If any means of escaping poverty presented itself
    that did not involve doing wrong, I would adopt it, even though
    my employment were only that of the gentleman who holds the
    whip.¹ But so long as it is a question of illegitimate means, I shall
    continue to pursue the quests that I love.²

12 The rites to which the Master gave the greatest attention were
    those connected with purification before sacrifice, with war and
    with sickness.³

13 When he was in Ch'i the Master heard the Succession,⁴ and for
    three months did not know the taste of meat.⁵ He said I did not
    picture to myself that any music existed which could reach such
    perfection as this.⁶

14 Jan Ch'iu said, Is our Master on the side of the Prince of Wei?⁷
    Tzu-kung said, Yes, I must ask him about that. He went in and
    said, What sort of people were Po I and Shu Ch'i?⁸ The Master
    said, They were good men who lived in the days of old. Tzu-
    kung said, Did they repine? The Master said, They sought
    Goodness and got Goodness. Why should they repine? On
    coming out Tzu-kung said, Our Master is not on his side.

1   i.e. the most menial. 'Gentleman', *shih*, in such contexts is used with
    a slightly ironical intention, as one might say in French 'le monsieur
    qui . . . ' cf. *Chuang Tzu* XV, 1.
2   The study of the Ancients.
3   A special sacrifice was held before the departure of military expeditions,
    and the sacrificial meat was distributed among the soldiers. The
    populace flocked to the Ancestral Shrines, wailing to the Ancestors for
    assistance. Sickness was exorcised by sacrifices to hills and streams.
4   See III, 25.
5   i.e. did not notice what he was eating.
6   The older commentators take 'this' to mean the land of Ch'i, i.e. 'I did
    not expect to find such music here in Ch'i.' This may be right.
7   When Duke Ling died in the summer of 493 BC the throne passed to
    his grandson, his son having previously abdicated his rights to the
    accession. Soon, however, the son went back on his word and
    attempted to oust the grandson from the throne.
8   See above, V, 22. The contrast is between Po I and Shu Ch'i on the
    one hand (they are always spoken of as though they were to all intents

15 The Master said, He who seeks only coarse food to eat, water to drink and a bent arm for pillow, will without looking for it find happiness to boot.[1] Any thought of accepting wealth and rank by means that I know to be wrong is as remote from me as the clouds that float above.

16 The Master said, Give me a few more years, so that I may have spent a whole fifty in study,[2] and I believe that after all I should be fairly free from error.

17 The occasions upon which the Master used correct pronunciation[3] were when reciting the *Songs* or the *Books* and when practising ritual acts. At all such times he used the correct pronunciation.

18 The 'Duke of Shê'[4] asked Tzu-lu about Master K'ung (Confucius). Tzu-lu did not reply. The Master said, Why did you not say 'This is the character of the man: so intent upon enlightening the eager that he forgets his hunger, and so happy in doing so, that he

---

and purposes a single person) and Duke Ling's son on the other. The two 'good men of old' harboured no rancour after their act of cession; whereas Ling's son became discontented with his lot. Tzu-kung sounds Confucius indirectly upon his attitude, because the Master was at this time living in Wei and would have been loath to make an open pronouncement on the question.

1 For the idiom, see II, 18.

2 In common with most scholars, I follow the Lu version here. The Ku version introduces a reference to the *Book of Changes*. But there is no reason to suppose that the *Changes* had in Confucius's time been philosophised, or that he regarded it as anything but a book of divination.

3 Whereas in daily life he used the Lu dialect. Similarly the Swiss, for example, use their own dialect in daily life, but Hochdeutsch in church services or in reciting a poem by Schiller. cf. *Hsün Tzu*, P'ien 4, A man of Yüeh is at ease in Yüeh speech, a man of Ch'u in Ch'u speech. They are gentlemen, in the 'correct pronunciation', *ya*, the same term as is used here. See further, additional notes.

4 An adventurer, known originally as Shên Chu-liang; first mentioned in 523 BC and still alive in 475. The title 'Duke of Shê' was one which he had invented for himself.

forgets the bitterness of his lot and does not realise that old age is at hand.[1] That is what he is.'

19 The Master said, I for my part[2] am not one of those who have innate knowledge. I am simply one who loves the past and who is diligent in investigating it.

20 The Master never talked of prodigies, feats of strength, disorders[3] or spirits.

21 The Master said, Even when walking in a party of no more than three I can always be certain of learning from those I am with. There will be good qualities that I can select for imitation and bad ones that will teach me what requires correction in myself.

22 The Master said, Heaven begat the power (te) that is in me. What have I to fear from such a one as Huan T'ui?[4]

23 The Master said, My friends, I know you think that there is something I am keeping from you. There is nothing at all that I keep from you. I take no steps about which I do not consult you, my friends. Were it otherwise, I should not be Ch'iu.[5]

24 The Master took four subjects for his teaching: culture, conduct of affairs, loyalty to superiors and the keeping of promises.

1 According to the traditional chronology Confucius was sixty-two at the time when this was said.
2 Wo, emphatic as opposed to the simple nominative wu. cf. Hu Shih Wên Ts'un, Vol. II, p. 13. cf. IV, 6 and note.
3 Disorders of nature; such as snow in summer, owls hooting by day, or the like.
4 Minister of War in Sung. cf. Tso Chuan, Duke Ai fourteenth year.
5 Familiar name of Confucius. There is no evidence that Confucius is here disclaiming the possession of an esoteric doctrine. The wording (hsing: steps, démarches) suggests that practical steps (with a view to office, patronage or the like) are all that is intended.

25 The Master said, A Divine Sage I cannot hope ever to meet; the most I can hope for is to meet a true gentleman. The Master said, A faultless man I cannot hope ever to meet; the most I can hope for is to meet a man of fixed principles. Yet where all around I see Nothing pretending to be Something,[1] Emptiness pretending to be Fullness, Penury pretending to be Affluence, even a man of fixed principles will be none too easy to find.

26 The Master fished with a line but not with a net; when fowling he did not aim at a roosting bird.[2]

27 The Master said, There may well be those who can do without knowledge; but I for my part am certainly not one of them. To hear much, pick out what is good and follow it, to see much and take due note of it,[3] is the lower[4] of the two kinds of knowledge.

28 At Hu village[5] the people were difficult to talk to.[6] But an uncapped[7] boy presented himself for an interview. The disciples were in two minds about showing him in. But the Master said, In sanctioning his entry here I am sanctioning nothing he may do when he retires. We must not be too particular. If anyone purifies[8] himself in order to come to us, let us accept this purification. We are not responsible for what he does when he goes away.

1 An impotent cipher pretending to be a Duke, powerless tools of adventurers such as Yang Huo pretending to be Ministers.
2 For 'fowling', see The Book of Songs, p. 36.
3 As I do.
4 The higher being innate knowledge, which Confucius disclaims above, VII, 19. He thus (ironically) places himself at two removes from the hypothetical people who can dispense with knowledge, the three stages being, (1) those who do not need knowledge; (2) those who have innate knowledge; (3) those who accumulate it by hard work.
5 Unknown. Probably one of the places Confucius passed through during his travels.
6 About the Way. cf. XV, 7.
7 The 'capping' of boys marked their initiation into manhood.
8 A suppliant of any kind (whether asking a Master for teaching or Heaven for good crops) purifies himself by fasting and abstinence in

29 The Master said, Is Goodness indeed so far away? If we really wanted Goodness, we should find that it was at our very side.

30 The Minister of Crime in Ch'ên asked whether Duke Chao of Lu knew the rites. Master K'ung said, He knew the rites. When Master K'ung had withdrawn, the Minister motioned Wu-ma Ch'i[1] to come forward and said, I have heard the saying 'A gentleman is never partial.' But it seems that some gentlemen are very partial indeed. His Highness[2] married into the royal family of Wu who belong to the same clan as himself, calling her Wu Mêng Tzu.[3] If his Highness knew the rites, who does not know the rites? Wu-ma Ch'i repeated this to the Master, who said, I am a fortunate man. If by any chance I make a mistake, people are certain to hear of it![4]

31 When in the Master's presence anyone sang a song that he liked, he did not join in at once, but asked for it to be repeated and then joined in.

32 The Master said, As far as taking trouble goes, I do not think I compare badly with other people. But as regards carrying out the duties of a gentleman in actual life, I have never yet had a chance to show what I could do.

33 The Master said, As to being a Divine Sage or even a Good Man, far be it from me to make any such claim. As for unwearying effort to learn and unflagging patience in teaching others,[5] those

---

order to enhance the power of his prayer. For abstinence before entertaining a teacher, cf. *Kuan Tzu*, P'ien 19, where the purification consists in washing in water from a new well, making a burnt offering, and ten days' abstinence and fasting.

1 Later regarded as a disciple of Confucius.

2 Duke Chao, reigned from 541 to 510 BC.

3 He broke the rule of exogamy and hoped to pass this off by speaking of her in a way that might lead people to think she belonged to another clan, the Tzu.

4 This is, of course, ironical. It would have been improper for Confucius to criticise his own late sovereign.

5 cf. *Mencius*, II, A, 2.

are merits that I do not hesitate to claim. Kung-hsi Hua said, The trouble is that we disciples cannot learn!

34   When the Master was very ill, Tzu-lu asked leave to perform the Rite of Expiation. The Master said, Is there such a thing?[1] Tzu-lu answered saying, There is. In one of the Dirges it says, 'We performed rites of expiation for you, calling upon the sky-spirits above and the earth-spirits below.' The Master said, My expiation began long ago![2]

35   The Master said, Just as lavishness leads easily to presumption, so does frugality to meanness. But meanness is a far less serious fault than presumption.[3]

36   The Master said, A true gentleman is calm and at ease; the Small Man is fretful and ill at ease.

37   The Master's manner was affable yet firm, commanding but not harsh, polite but easy.

1   i.e. is there any ancient authority for such a rite?

2   What justifies me in the eyes of Heaven is the life I have led. There is no need for any rite now. In a fragment of one of the lost books of *Chuang Tzu* there is a parallel story in which Tzu-lu wants to take the omens about Confucius's chance of recovery, and Confucius says 'My omen-taking was done long ago!' See *T'ai P'ing Yü Lan* 849, fol. I verso. The reference was kindly sent to me by Dr Gustav Haloun.

3   cf. III, 4. The lavishness of the Chi Family became presumption when it led them to have eight rows of dancers (III, 1) and thereby infringe upon a ducal prerogative.

BOOK EIGHT

1 The Master said, Of T'ai Po[1] it may indeed be said that he attained to the very highest pitch of moral power. No less than three times he renounced the sovereignty of all things under Heaven, without the people getting a chance to praise him for it.

2 The Master said, Courtesy not bounded by the prescriptions of ritual becomes tiresome. Caution not bounded by the prescriptions of ritual becomes timidity, daring becomes turbulence, inflexibility becomes harshness.[2]

The Master said,[3] When gentlemen deal generously with their own kin, the common people are incited to Goodness. When old dependents are not discarded, the common people will not be fickle.

1 T'ai Po was the eldest son of King Tan, legendary ancestor of the Chou sovereigns. He renounced the Throne in favour of his youngest brother. *Jang* (renunciation) is the virtue that engenders the greatest quantity of *te* (moral power). No renunciation can be greater than to renounce 'the sovereignty of all things under Heaven'. Moreover, a *yin te* (secret accretion of 'power) is always more redoubtable than an open one. The secrecy seems to have been achieved by giving it out that T'ai Po's flight to the lands of Wu and Yüeh was undertaken in order to collect medicines for Old King Tan, who was ill. (Chêng Hsüan makes a rather forced effort to enumerate three separate occasions upon which T'ai Po renounced his claims.)

2 Compare XVII, 8.

3 The Pelliot MS. supplies these words, which have dropped out of the current version.

3   When Master Tsêng was ill he summoned his disciples and said,
     Free my feet, free my hands. The *Song* says:

> In fear and trembling,
> With caution and care,
> As though on the brink of a chasm,
> As though treading thin ice.

But I feel now that whatever may betide I have got through
safely, my little ones.[1]

4   When Master Tsêng was ill, Mêng Ching Tzu[2] came to see him.
     Master Tsêng spoke to him saying, When a bird is about to die
     its song touches the heart.[3] When a man is about to die, his
     words are of note. There are three things that a gentleman, in
     following the Way, places above all the rest: from every attitude,
     every gesture that he employs he must remove all trace of
     violence or arrogance; every look that he composes in his face
     must betoken good faith; from every word that he utters, from
     every intonation, he must remove all trace of coarseness or
     impropriety. As to the ordering of ritual vessels and the like, there
     are those whose business it is to attend to such matters.

5   Master Tsêng said, Clever, yet not ashamed to consult those less
     clever than himself; widely gifted, yet not ashamed to consult
     those with few gifts; having, yet seeming not to have; full, yet
     seeming empty; offended against, yet never contesting – long ago
     I had a friend[4] whose ways were such as this.

1   While a man was dying four people held his hands and feet, 'one for
     each limb' (*Li Chi*, XXII). After death, the hands and feet were freed (*Li
     I Chih*, supplement to the *Hou Han Shu*, Part III, fol. 1). Tsêng says that
     he has got through safely, his moral course is run; there is no need to
     hold his hands and feet, which was done 'in case the dying man should
     in his death-struggle get into some "non-ritual" attitude'. He interprets
     the *Song* 295 as describing the heavy responsibilities of the man who has
     'taken Goodness for his load'; see below, VIII, 7. For the anthropological
     connotations of 'freeing hands and feet', see additional notes.

2   Son of Mêng Wu Po (see II, 6). He appears to have been still alive in
     430 BC.

3   cf. our belief concerning 'swan-songs'.

4   It has been suggested that the friend in question was Yen Hui.

6 Master Tsêng said, The man to whom one could with equal confidence entrust an orphan not yet fully grown[1] or the sovereignty of a whole State,[2] whom the advent of no emergency however great could upset – would such a one be a true gentleman? He I think would be a true gentleman indeed.

7 Master Tsêng said, The true Knight of the Way must perforce be both broad-shouldered and stout of heart; his burden is heavy and he has far to go. For Goodness is the burden he has taken upon himself; and must we not grant that it is a heavy one to bear? Only with death does his journey end; then must we not grant that he has far to go?

8 The Master said, Let a man be first incited by the *Songs,* then given a firm footing by the study of ritual, and finally perfected by music.

9 The Master said, The common people can be made to follow it;[3] they cannot be made to understand it.

10 The Master said, One who is by nature daring and is suffering from poverty will not long be law-abiding. Indeed, any men, save those that are truly Good, if their sufferings are very great, will be likely to rebel.[4]

11 The Master said, If a man has gifts as wonderful as those of the Duke of Chou, yet is arrogant and mean, all the rest is of no account.

12 The Master said:

> One who will study for three years
> Without thought of reward[5]
> Would be hard indeed to find.

---

1 Literally, an orphan of six feet (i.e. four of our feet).
2 Literally, the command of a hundred leagues.
3 i.e. the Way.
4 Official interpretation, 'Men who are not truly Good, if you criticise them too severely, are likely to rebel.'
5 i.e. of obtaining a paid appointment.

13   The Master said, Be of unwavering good faith, love learning, if attacked[1] be ready to die for the good Way. Do not enter a State that pursues dangerous courses, nor stay in one where the people have rebelled. When the Way prevails under Heaven, then show yourself; when it does not prevail, then hide. When the Way prevails in your own land, count it a disgrace to be needy and obscure; when the Way does not prevail in your land, then count it a disgrace to be rich and honoured.

14   The Master said, He who holds no rank in a State does not discuss its policies.

15   The Master said, When Chih the Chief Musician led the climax of the *Ospreys*,[2] what a grand flood of sound filled one's ears!

16   The Master said, Impetuous, but tricky! Ingenuous, but dishonest! Simple-minded, but capable of breaking promises![3] To such men I can give no recognition.

17   The Master said, Learn as if you were following someone whom you could not catch up, as though it were someone you were frightened of losing.

18   The Master said, Sublime were Shun and Yü! All that is under Heaven was theirs, yet they remained aloof from it.

19   The Master said, Greatest, as lord and ruler, was Yao.[4] Sublime, indeed, was he. 'There is no greatness like the greatness of Heaven', yet Yao could copy it. So boundless was it[5] that the people could find no name for it;[6] yet sublime were his achievements, dazzling the insignia of his culture!

---

1   Literally, 'on the defensive'.
2   See III, 20. For Chih, see XVIII, 9.
3   In old days (see XVII, 16) people at any rate had the merits of their faults.
4   cf. *Mencius*, III, A, 4.
5   i.e. Yao's *te*.
6   So that it remained a *yin te* (secret prestige). cf. above, VIII, 1.

20 Shun had five ministers and all that is under Heaven was well
ruled. King Wu[1] said, I have ten[2] ministers. Master K'ung said,
True indeed is the saying that 'the right material is hard to find';
for the turn of the T'ang and Yü dynasties[3] was the time most
famous for this.[4] (As for King Wu),[5] there was a woman among
his ten, so that in reality there were only nine men. Yet of all that
is under Heaven he held two parts in three, using them in
submissive service to the dynasty of Yin.[6] The moral power (te)
of Chou may, indeed, be called an absolutely perfect moral
power!

21 The Master said, In Yü I can find no semblance of a flaw.
Abstemious in his own food and drink, he displayed the utmost
devotion in his offerings to spirits and divinities.[7] Content with
the plainest clothes for common wear, he saw to it that his
sacrificial apron and ceremonial head–dress were of the utmost
magnificence. His place of habitation was of the humblest, and all
his energy went into draining and ditching. In him I can find no
semblance of a flaw.

1　The Warrior King, founder of the Chou dynasty.

2　His mother, and his nine brothers? See additional notes.

3　i.e. the accession of Shun.

4　i.e. for 'the right material', for an abundance of good ministers. Yet
even then there were only five.

5　Some such words have dropped out of the text.

6　And by this act of cession (jang) building up the te required for his
subsequent campaign. For the whole paragraph, see additional notes.

7　To ancestors, and spirits of hill, stream, etc.

BOOK NINE

1 The Master seldom spoke of profit or fate or Goodness.[1]

2 A villager from Ta-hsiang said, Master K'ung is no doubt a very great man and vastly learned. But he does nothing to bear out this reputation. The Master, hearing of it, said to his disciples, What shall I take up? Shall I take up chariot-driving? Or shall it be archery? I think I will take up driving![2]

3 The Master said, The hemp-thread crown is prescribed by ritual.[3] Nowadays people wear black silk, which is economical; and I follow the general practice. Obeisance below the daïs is prescribed by ritual. Nowadays people make obeisance after mounting the daïs. This is presumptuous, and though to do so is contrary to the general practice, I make a point of bowing while still down below.

4 There were four things that the Master wholly eschewed: he took nothing for granted,[4] he was never over-positive, never obstinate, never egotistic.

1 We may expand: Seldom spoke of matters from the point of view of what would pay best, but only from the point of view of what was right. He did not discuss whether Heaven determines all human actions (a question debated by the school of Mo Tzu in later days and evidently already raised in the time of Confucius). He refused to define Goodness or accord the title Good to any of his contemporaries.

2 See additional notes.

3 For wear at the ancestral sacrifice; made of threads twisted from a very thin yarn, very costly to manufacture.

4 Chêng Hsüan (Pelliot MS.) reads the 'man' determinative at the side of

5   When the Master was trapped in K'uang,[1] he said, When King
    Wên perished, did that mean that culture (wên) ceased to exist?[2]
    If Heaven had really intended that such culture as his should
    disappear, a latter-day mortal would never have been able to link
    himself to it as I have done. And if Heaven does not intend to
    destroy such culture, what have I to fear from the people of
    K'uang?

6   The Grand Minister (of Wu?)[3] asked Tzu-kung saying, Is your
    Master a Divine Sage? If so, how comes it that he has many
    practical accomplishments?[4] Tzu kung said, Heaven certainly
    intended[5] him to become a Sage; it is also true that he has many
    accomplishments. When the Master heard of it he said, The
    Grand Minister is quite right about me. When I was young I was
    in humble circumstances; that is why I have many practical
    accomplishments in regard to simple, everyday matters. Does it
    befit a gentleman to have many accomplishments? No, he is in
    no need of them at all.
    Lao says that the Master said, It is because I have not been
    given a chance[6] that I have become so handy.

---

i and interprets 'he never took anything for granted when he was not
sure'. This is certainly right.

1   A border town held at various times by Chêng, Wei, Sung and Lu. For
    the legend as to why he was maltreated here, see additional notes.

2   Literally, 'was not in this'. cf. the common Chinese phrase 'Suppose
    there were a man in this', i.e. 'suppose the case of a man who . . . ',
    'being in this' meaning 'existing'. cf. Mencius, VI, B, 2. 'Take the case of
    a man not strong enough to lift . . . '

3   Probably P'i (adult name, Tzu-yü), who is mentioned in connection
    with Tzu-kung in 488 BC.

4   Gentlemen do not stoop to practical accomplishments; much less the
    Sage.

5   But the wickedness of the world prevented it.

6   In public life. Lao is usually identified with the Ch'in Chang
    mentioned in Tso Chuan, Duke Chao, 20th year, and the Tzu-lao of
    Chuang Tzu XXV, 6.

7   The Master said, Do I regard myself as a possessor of wisdom? Far from it. But if even a simple peasant comes in all sincerity and asks me a question, I am ready to thrash the matter out, with all its pros and cons, to the very end.

8   The Master said, The phoenix does not come; the river gives forth no chart.[1] It is all over with me![2]

9   Whenever he was visited by anyone dressed in the robes of mourning or wearing ceremonial headdress, with gown and skirt, or a blind man, even if such a one were younger than himself, the Master on seeing him invariably rose to his feet, and if compelled to walk past him always quickened his step.[3]

10   Yen Hui said with a deep sigh, The more I strain my gaze up towards it,[4] the higher it soars. The deeper I bore down into it, the harder it becomes. I see it in front; but suddenly it is behind. Step by step the Master skilfully lures one on. He has broadened me with culture, restrained me with ritual. Even if I wanted to stop, I could not. Just when I feel that I have exhausted every resource, something seems to rise up, standing out sharp and clear.[5] Yet though I long to pursue it, I can find no way of getting to it at all.

11   When the Master was very ill, Tzu-lu caused some of the disciples to get themselves up as official retainers.[6] Coming to himself for a short while, the Master said, How like Yu, to go in for this sort of imposture! In pretending to have retainers when I have none, whom do I deceive? Do I deceive Heaven? Not only would I far rather die in the arms of you disciples than in the arms of retainers, but also as regards my funeral – even if I am not accorded a State Burial, it is not as though I were dying by the roadside.[7]

1   The arrival of this magical bird and the sudden revelation of a magical chart were portents that heralded the rise of a Saviour Sage.

2   Heaven does not intend to let me play a Sage's part.

3   A sign of respect.

4   Goodness.

5   Literally, 'overtoppingly', like a mountain-top or the top of a tree.

6   Such as he would have been entitled to, had he held office.

7   i.e. don't think I am worrying about whether I shall be buried with

12 Tzu-kung said, Suppose one had a lovely jewel, should one wrap it up, put it in a box and keep it, or try to get the best price one can for it? The Master said, Sell it! Most certainly sell it! I myself am one who is waiting for an offer.[1]

13 The Master wanted to settle among the Nine Wild Tribes of the East.[2] Someone said, I am afraid you would find it hard to put up with their lack of refinement. The Master said, Were a true gentleman to settle among them there would soon be no trouble[3] about lack of refinement.

14 The Master said, It was only after my return from Wei to Lu that music was revised, Court pieces and Ancestral Recitations being at last properly discriminated.[4]

15 The Master said, I can claim that at Court I have duly served the Duke and his officers; at home, my father and elder brother. As regards matters of mourning, I am conscious of no neglect, nor have I ever been overcome with wine. Concerning these things at any rate my mind is quite at rest.[5]

16 Once when the Master was standing by a stream, he said, Could one but go on and on[6] like this, never ceasing day or night!

17 The Master said, I have never yet seen anyone whose desire to build up his moral power was as strong as sexual desire.

---

public honours. I know I can trust you to give me a decent burial; and that is all I ask for.

1 The question at issue is, of course, whether a man of talent should try to obtain office. Confucius declares that he himself is only too anxious to 'sell his jewel' (i.e. accept office), should any opportunity present itself.

2 For Confucius's ideas on the 'noble savage', see V, 6 and note.

3 For *ho yu*, an idiom that cannot be translated literally, cf. VI, 6, VII, 2, IX, 15.

4 The words of the Court pieces (*ya*) are contained in the second and third parts, the Recitations (*sung*) in the last of the four great divisions of the *Book of Songs*.

5 Another instance of the idiomatic *ho yu*.

6 In one's moral striving, cf. *Mencius*, IV, B, 18

18 The Master said, The case[1] is like that of someone raising a mound. If he stops working, the fact that it perhaps needed only one more basketful makes no difference; I stay where I am. Whereas even if he has not got beyond levelling the ground, but is still at work, the fact that he has only tilted one basketful of earth makes no difference. I go to help him.

19 The Master said, It was Hui whom I could count on always to listen attentively to anything I said.

20 The Master said of Yen Hui, Alas, I saw him go forward, but had no chance to see whither this progress would have led him in the end.[2]

21 The Master said, There are shoots whose lot it is to spring up but never to flower; others whose lot it is to flower, but never bear fruit.[3]

22 The Master said, Respect the young. How do you know that they will not one day be all that you are now? But if a man has reached forty or fifty and nothing has been heard of him, then I grant there is no need to respect him.

23 The Master said, The words of the *Fa Yü*[4] (Model Sayings) cannot fail to stir us; but what matters is that they should change our ways. The words of the *Hsüan Chü*[5] cannot fail to commend themselves to us; but what matters is that we should carry them out. For those who approve but do not carry out, who are stirred, but do not change, I can do nothing at all.

1   i.e. my attitude towards disciples in different stages of progress. A parallel passage in *Hsün Tzu* P'ien 28, makes the sense and construction of this passage quite clear.

2   This seems better than the traditional, 'I saw him make progress and never saw him stand still.'

3   This surely refers to Yen Hui's early death.

4   Name of a collection of moral sayings? I suspect that it is the same as the *Fa Yen* twice quoted in *Chuang Tzu* (IV, 2).

5   Name of another collection of moral sayings, on the 'choice' and 'promotion' of the virtuous?

24 The Master said, First and foremost, be faithful to your superiors, keep all promises, refuse the friendship of all who are not like you; and if you have made a mistake, do not be afraid of admitting the fact and amending your ways.[1]

25 The Master said, You may rob the Three Armies of their commander-in-chief, but you cannot deprive the humblest peasant of his opinion.

26 The Master said, 'Wearing a shabby hemp-quilted gown, yet capable of standing unabashed with those who wore fox and badger.' That would apply quite well to Yu, would it not?

> Who harmed none, was foe to none,
> Did nothing that was not right.[2]

Afterwards Tzu-lu (Yu) kept on continually chanting those lines to himself. The Master said, Come now, the wisdom contained in them is not worth treasuring[3] to that extent!

27 The Master said,[4] Only when the year grows cold do we see that the pine and cypress are the last[5] to fade.

28 The Master said, He that is really Good can never be unhappy. He that is really wise can never be perplexed. He that is really brave is never afraid.[6]

1   cf. I, 8.
2   Confucius quotes these two lines from *Songs*, No. 67.
3   Pun on two senses of *tsang* (1) excellent; (2) treasure, to treasure up, to store.
4   He is, however, only repeating a proverb.
5   *hou* (last) should probably be *pu* or *wu* (not). A similar saying in *Lü Shih Ch'un Ch'iu* (74, 2) refers to the Master's ordeals in Ch'ên and Ts'ai. cf. *Chuang Tzu* XXVIII, 8.
6   Goodness, wisdom and courage are the Three Ways of the true gentleman. cf. XIV, 30. Confucius always ranks courage below wisdom and wisdom below Goodness. In the original the first two clauses have become transposed. This is, however, a mere slip, as is shown by comparison with the parallel passage, XIV, 30. The *Chung Yung* (*Doctrine of the Mean*), XX, in reproducing the terms in the order wisdom, goodness, courage, merely betrays the influence of this corrupted passage.

29 The Master said, There are some whom one can join in study but whom one cannot join in progress along the Way; others whom one can join in progress along the Way, but beside whom one cannot take one's stand;[1] and others again beside whom one can take one's stand, but whom one cannot join in counsel.

30   The flowery branch of the wild cherry

How swiftly it flies back![2]
It is not that I do not love you;
But your house is far away.

The Master said, He did not really love her. Had he done so, he would not have worried about the distance.[3]

---

1 i.e. with whom one cannot collaborate in office. cf. X, 3 and XVI, 13.
2 When one pulls it to pluck the blossom. cf. *Songs*, 268, 1. Image of things that are torn apart after a momentary union. Evidently a verse from some song not included in our *Book of Songs*.
3 Men fail to attain to Goodness because they do not care for it sufficiently, not because Goodness 'is far away'. I think the old interpretation, which treats 29 and 30 as one paragraph, is definitely wrong.

BOOK TEN

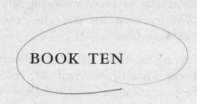

1   At home in his native village his manner is simple and unassuming, as though he did not trust himself to speak. But in the ancestral temple and at Court he speaks readily, though always choosing his words with care.

2   At Court when conversing with the Under Ministers his attitude is friendly and affable; when conversing with the Upper Ministers, it is restrained and formal. When the ruler is present it is wary, but not cramped.

3   When the ruler summons him to receive a guest, a look of confusion comes over his face and his legs seem to give beneath his weight. When saluting his colleagues he passes his right hand to the left, letting his robe hang down in front and behind; and as he advances with quickened step, his attitude is one of majestic dignity.

    When the guest has gone, he reports the close of the visit, saying, 'The guest is no longer looking back.'

4   On entering the Palace Gate he seems to shrink into himself, as though there were not room. If he halts, it must never be in the middle of the gate, nor in going through does he ever tread on the threshold. As he passes the Stance[1] a look of confusion comes over his face, his legs seem to give way under him and words seem to fail him. While, holding up the hem of his skirt, he ascends the Audience Hall, he seems to double up and keeps in his breath, so that you would think he was not breathing at all.

1   The place where the ruler takes up his stand when seeing off important guests?

On coming out, after descending the first step his expression relaxes into one of satisfaction and relief. At the bottom of the steps he quickens his pace, advancing with an air of majestic dignity. On regaining his place he resumes his attitude of wariness and hesitation.

5   When carrying the tablet of jade,[1] he seems to double up, as though borne down by its weight. He holds it at the highest as though he were making a bow,[2] at the lowest, as though he were proffering a gift. His expression, too, changes to one of dread and his feet seem to recoil, as though he were avoiding something. When presenting ritual-presents, his expression is placid. At the private audience his attitude is gay and animated.

6   A gentleman does not wear facings of purple or mauve, nor in undress does he use pink or roan.[3] In hot weather he wears an unlined gown of fine thread loosely woven, but puts on an outside garment before going out-of-doors.[4] With a black robe he wears black lambskin; with a robe of undyed silk, fawn. With a yellow robe, fox fur.[5] On his undress robe the fur cuffs are long; but the right is shorter than the left.[6] His bedclothes must be half as long again as a man's height.[7] The thicker kinds of fox and badger are for home wear. Except when in mourning, he wears all his girdle-ornaments.[8] Apart from his Court apron, all his

1   Symbol of the ruler's feudal investiture; the *kuei*.
2   On a level with his forehead.
3   Usually translated 'purple'. But the term is applied to the coats of horses and cannot mean anything that we should call purple. These colours were reserved for times of fasting and mourning.
4   To do otherwise would be like going out into the town in one's shirt-sleeves.
5   cf. our black tie with black waistcoat.
6   To give him freedom of movement (pseudo K'ung An-kuo).
7   He does not, of course, undress, but simply draws the bedclothes over him. According to Chu Hsi this refers only to one preparing for sacrifice.
8   Which are lucky talismans; or (in a more sophisticated vein of explanations) symbolic ornaments indicating his rank. Those of an ordinary gentleman were of jade.

skirts are wider at the bottom than at the waist. Lambskin dyed black and a hat of dark-dyed silk must not be worn when making visits of condolence.[1] At the Announcement of the New Moon he must go to Court in full Court dress.

7, 8.   When preparing himself for sacrifice he must wear the Bright Robe,[2] and it must be of linen. He must change his food and also the place where he commonly sits. But there is no objection to his rice being of the finest quality, nor to his meat being finely minced. Rice affected by the weather or turned he must not eat, nor fish that is not sound, nor meat that is high. He must not eat anything discoloured or that smells bad. He must not eat what is overcooked nor what is undercooked, nor anything that is out of season. He must not eat what has been crookedly cut, nor any dish that lacks its proper seasoning. The meat that he eats must at the very most not be enough to make his breath smell of meat rather than of rice. As regards wine, no limit is laid down; but he must not be disorderly. He may not drink wine bought at a shop or eat dried meat from the market. He need not refrain from such articles of food as have ginger sprinkled over them; but he must not eat much of such dishes.[3]

After a sacrifice in the ducal palace, the flesh must not be kept overnight. No sacrificial flesh may be kept beyond the third day. If it is kept beyond the third day, it may no longer be eaten. While it is being eaten, there must be no conversation, nor any word spoken while lying down after the repast. Any article of food, whether coarse rice, vegetables, broth or melon, that has been used as an offering must be handled with due solemnity.

9   He must not sit on a mat that is not straight.[4]

10   When the men of his village are drinking wine he leaves the feast directly the village-elders have left. When the men of his village

---

1   i.e., 'plain' articles must be worn, approximating to those worn by the mourner. For these rules of dress, cf. *Li Chi*, XIII, fol. 3.

2   *Ming I*, the 'spirit robe' used during the period of purification. cf. *Ming Ch'i*, 'spirit gear', the objects buried along with the dead in a tomb.

3   All the above refers to periods of preparation for sacrifice.

4   While eating sacrificial flesh?

hold their Expulsion Rite,[1] he puts on his Court dress and stands on the eastern steps.[2]

11 When sending a messenger to enquire after someone in another country, he prostrates himself twice while speeding the messenger on his way. When K'ang-tzu[3] sent him some medicine he prostrated himself and accepted it; but said, As I am not acquainted with its properties, I cannot venture to taste it.[4]

12 When the stables were burnt down, on returning from Court, he said, Was anyone hurt? He did not ask about the horses.

13 When his prince sends him a present of food, he[5] must straighten his mat and be the first to taste what has been sent. When what his prince sends is a present of uncooked meat, he must cook it and make a sacrificial offering. When his prince sends a live animal, he must rear it.[6] When he is waiting upon his prince at meal-times, while his prince is making the sacrificial offering, he (the gentleman) tastes the dishes. If he is ill and his prince comes to see him, he has himself laid with his head to the East with his Court robes thrown over him and his sash drawn across the bed. When the prince commands his presence he goes straight to the palace without waiting for his carriage to be yoked.[7]

14 On entering the Ancestral Temple, he asks about every detail.[8]

15 If a friend dies and there are no relatives to fall back on, he says, 'The funeral is my affair.' On receiving a present from a friend, even a carriage and horses, he does not prostrate himself. He does so only in the case of sacrificial meat being sent.

---

1   The driving away of evil spirits at the close of the year; see additional notes.

2   The place occupied by one who is presiding over a ceremony.

3   Head of the all-powerful Chi family. This sentence and the next paragraph obviously refer to Confucius himself.

4   A *chün-tzu* takes no medicine except that administered to him by a doctor whose father and grandfather have served the family. Compare the attachment of the English *chün-tzu* to the 'old family doctor'.

5   The gentleman?   6   Not use it for food.

7   cf. *Mencius*, V, B, 7.   8   cf. III, 15.

16 In bed he avoids lying in the posture of a corpse.[1] When at home he does not use ritual attitudes. When appearing before[2] anyone in mourning, however well he knows him, he must put on an altered expression, and when appearing before anyone in sacrificial garb, or a blind man, even informally, he must be sure to adopt the appropriate attitude. On meeting anyone in deep mourning he must bow across the bar of his chariot; he also bows to people carrying planks.[3] When confronted with a particularly choice dainty at a banquet, his countenance should change and he should rise to his feet. Upon hearing a sudden clap of thunder or a violent gust of wind, he must change countenance.

17 When mounting a carriage, he must stand facing it squarely and holding the mounting-cord. When riding he confines his gaze,[4] does not speak rapidly or point with his hands.[5]

18 (The gentleman) rises and goes at the first sign,[6] and does not 'settle till he has hovered'.[7] (A song) says:

> The hen-pheasant of the hill-bridge,
> Knows how to bide its time, to bide its time!
> When Tzu-lu made it an offering,
> It sniffed three times before it rose.[8]

1 i.e. with his face to the North, where lies the land of the Dead.
2 Or 'when he sees'. For different ways of writing the expression for 'mourning garb', see *Tz'u T'ung*, 434.
3 Traditionally explained as meaning 'census tablets'.
4 Does not look about promiscuously.
5 Pointing is considered maleficent, unlucky, rude, as the case may be, in many parts of the world.
6 Of evil intentions on the part of the ruler; cf. *Lü Shih Ch'un Ch'iu*, P'ien 101, fol. 1. 'The *chün-tzu* is like a bird; if he is startled he rises.'
7 Is circumspect in choosing a new State in which to settle.
8 This quatrain (if such it is intended to be) resembles in content the songs by means of which the people commented on current political events. It is natural to interpret it as referring to the circumspect conduct of Confucius when the Chi Family (through the agency of Tzu-lu) invited him to return to Lu. One makes an offering to birds or animals whose behaviour suggests that they are sent by Heaven as omens or portents. For an anecdote of Tzu-lu and a pheasant, see *Lü Shih Ch'un Ch'iu*, 44, 1.

BOOK ELEVEN

1   The Master said, 'Only common people wait till they are
    advanced in ritual and music [before taking office]. A gentleman
    can afford to get up his ritual and music later on.' Even if I
    accepted this saying, I should still be on the side of those who get
    on with their studies first.[1]

2a The Master said, My adherents in Ch'ên and Ts'ai were none of
    them in public service.[2]

2b Those who worked by moral power were Yen Hui, Min Tzu-
    ch'ien, Jan Kêng and Jan Yung. Those who spoke well were Tsai
    Yü and Tzu-kung. Those who surpassed in handling public
    business were Jan Ch'iu and Tzu-lu; in culture and learning,
    Tzu-yu and Tzu-hsia.[3]

3   The Master said, Hui was not any help to me; he accepted
    everything I said.

---

1   This is the interpretation of Liu Pao-nan, founded on Chêng Hsüan.
    For the contrast between *chün-tzu* and *yeh-jen* cf. *Mencius*, III, A, 3: 'If
    there were no *chün-tzu*, there would be no one to keep the common
    people (*yeh-jen*) in order; if there were no common people, there
    would be no one to produce food for the *chün-tzu*.'

2   cf. *Mencius*, VII, B, 18, where Confucius's difficulties in Ch'ên and Ts'ai
    are attributed to his being out of touch with the ruling classes in those
    States. The current interpretation 'Not one of them now comes near
    my door', taken as a complaint of their infidelity, is comparatively
    recent.

3   This classification of the disciples is not put into the mouth of
    Confucius, as is clear from the form in which the names are given.

4 The Master said, Min Tzu-ch'ien is indeed a very good son. No one can take exception to what his parents or brothers have said of him.[1]

5 Nan Jung in reciting the *I* Song repeated the verse about the sceptre of white jade three times. (In consequence of which) Master K'ung gave him his elder brother's daughter to marry.[2]

6 K'ang-tzu of the Chi Family asked which of the disciples had a love of learning. Master K'ung replied, There was Yen Hui. He was fond of learning, but unfortunately his allotted span was a short one, and he died. Now there is none.

7 When Yen Hui died, his father Yen Lu begged for the Master's carriage, that he might use it to make the enclosure[3] for the coffin. The Master said, Gifted or not gifted,[4] you have spoken of your son and I will now speak of mine. When Li[5] died he had a coffin, but no enclosure. I did not go on foot in order that he might have an enclosure; for I rank next to the Great Officers[6] and am not permitted to go on foot.

8 When Yen Hui died, the Master said, Alas, Heaven has bereft me, Heaven has bereft me![7]

9 When Yen Hui died the Master wailed without restraint. His followers said, Master, you are wailing without restraint! He said, Am I doing so? Well, if any man's death could justify abandoned wailing, it would surely be this man's!

1 For the legend of his piety, see additional notes.
2 The Song in question is No. 271; see verse 5: A flaw in a white jade sceptre may be polished away; but a flaw in words cannot be repaired. 'Gave him his brother's daughter,' cf. V, 1.
3 See additional notes.
4 Confucius thus apologises for putting his son on a level with Yen Hui.
5 The name means 'carp-fish'. Later tradition makes him die later than Yen Hui.
6 It was the *shih* (knights, gentlemen, those who fought in chariots and not afoot) who ranked after the Great Officers, and it is possible that Confucius ranked as 'leader of the *shih*'.
7 Recorded because Confucius rarely spoke of Heaven?

10 When Yen Hui died, the disciples wanted to give him a grand burial. The Master said it would be wrong to do so; nevertheless they gave him a grand burial. The Master said, Hui dealt with me as though I were his father. But I have failed to deal with him as though he were my son.[1] The fault however is not mine. It is yours, my friends!

11 Tzu-lu asked how one should serve ghosts and spirits. The Master said, Till you have learnt to serve men, how can you serve ghosts? Tzu-lu then ventured upon a question about the dead. The Master said, Till you know about the living, how are you to know about the dead?[2]

12a When Min Tzu-ch'ien stood by the Master's side in attendance upon him his attitude was one of polite restraint. That of Tzu-lu was one of impatient energy; that of Jan Ch'iu and of Tzu-kung was genial and affable. The Master was pleased.

12b [The Master said],[3] A man like Yu[4] never dies in his bed.

13 When the men of Lu were dealing with the question of the Long Treasury, Min Tzu-ch'ien said, What about restoring it on the old lines? I see no necessity for rebuilding it on a new plan.[5] The Master said, That man is no talker; but when he does say anything, he invariably hits the mark.

14 The Master said, Yu's zithern has no right to be in my house at all.[6] Whereupon the disciples ceased to respect Tzu-lu. The

1 Failed to assert my right to bury him in the way I thought suitable.
2 e.g. whether they are conscious, which was a much debated problem.
3 There seems to be a hiatus in the text.
4 Tzu-lu. For his death in 480 BC during the accession struggles in Wei, see *Tso Chuan*, Ai kung, 15th year. Confucius may well have said this on hearing of Tzu-lu's death. The words are usually regarded as a prophecy.
5 The point of the remark is very uncertain. See additional notes.
6 i.e. Tzu-lu has no right to call himself a follower of my Way. The *sê* was a 25-stringed zithern.

Master said, The truth about Yu is that he has got as far as the guest-hall, but has not yet entered the inner rooms.[1]

15 Tzu-kung asked which was the better, Shih or Shang.[2] The Master said, Shih goes too far and Shang does not go far enough. Tzu-kung said, If that is so, then Shih excels. The Master said, To go too far is as bad as not to go far enough.

16 The head of the Chi Family was richer than the Duke of Chou;[3] but Ch'iu,[4] when entrusted with the task of collecting his revenues for him, added to them and increased the yield. The Master said, He is no follower of mine. My little ones, you may beat the drum and set upon him. I give you leave.[5]

17 [The Master said], Ch'ai[6] is stupid, Shên[7] is dull-witted, Shih[8] is too formal; Yu, too free and easy.[9]

---

1 Tzu-lu had an abundance of courage, which is the elementary virtue of the gentleman. But he lacked the two other virtues: wisdom and Goodness.

2 i.e. Tzu-chang or Tzu-hsia.

3 Huang K'an (sixth century) says that this does not refer to Tan, legendary founder of Lu, but to a subsequent Duke of Chou. cf. however, Hsün Tzu, P'ien, 8, fol. 5, where the wealth of Tan is referred to.

4 i.e. Jan Ch'iu. The form in which the name is given suggests that these words were spoken by Confucius or a disciple and are not a statement of the compiler's.

5 This is, of course, meant metaphorically. The same anecdote occurs in Mencius, IV, A, 14.

6 Kao Ch'ai, associated with Tzu-lu in the Wei accession troubles.

7 Master Tsêng.

8 Tzu-chang. The meaning of the epithet p'i is very uncertain. See textual notes. Chu Hsi's 'it means that he was expert in ritual attitudes and deportment, but lacked sincerity' is not a philological gloss on p'i, but an application to this passage of what is said about Tzu-chang in XIX, 16.

9 Tradition represents Tzu-lu as a converted swashbuckler. See textual notes.

18 The Master said, Hui comes very near to it.[1] He is often empty.[2] Ssu (Tzu-kung) was discontented with his lot and has taken steps to enrich himself.[3] In his calculations he often hits the mark.

19 Tzu-chang asked about the Way of the good people.[4] The Master said, He who does not tread in the tracks[5] cannot expect to find his way into the Inner Room.

20 The Master said (of someone), That his conversation is sound one may grant. But whether he is indeed a true gentleman or merely one who adopts outward airs of solemnity, it is not so easy to say.

21 Tzu-lu asked, When one hears a maxim, should one at once seek occasion to put it into practice? The Master said, Your father and elder brother are alive. How can you whenever you hear a maxim at once put it into practice? Jan Ch'iu asked, When one hears a maxim, should one at once seek occasion to put it into practice? The Master said, When one hears it, one should at once put it into practice.

Kung-hsi Hua said, When Yu asked, 'When one hears a maxim, should one at once put it into practice?' you said, You have a father and elder brother alive. But when Ch'iu asked, 'When one hears a maxim, should one at once put it into practice,' you said, 'When you hear it, put it into practice.' I am perplexed, and would venture to ask how this was. The Master said, Ch'iu is backward; so I urged him on. Yu is fanatical about Goodness; so I held him back.

22 When the Master was trapped in K'uang,[6] Yen Hui fell behind. The Master said, I thought you were dead. Hui said, While you are alive how should I dare to die?

---

1 To Goodness. The rest of the paragraph runs very awkwardly and is probably corrupt.
2 Hard up.
3 'Traded without official permission' is a possible interpretation.
4 Possibly a rival Way to that of Confucius.
5 Of the Ancients.
6 See above, IX, 5. The story is also found in *Lü Shih Ch'un Ch'iu*, 17.

23 Chi Tzu-jan[1] asked whether Tzu-lu and Jan Ch'iu could be called great ministers. The Master said, I thought you were going to ask some really interesting question; and it is after all only a question about Yu and Ch'iu! What I call a great minister is one who will only serve his prince while he can do so without infringement of the Way, and as soon as this is impossible, resigns. But in the present case, so far as concerns Yu and Ch'iu, I should merely call them stop-gap ministers. Tzu-jan said, So you think they would merely do what they were told? The Master said, If called upon to slay their father or their prince, even *they* would refuse.

24 Tzu-lu got Kao Ch'ai made Warden of Pi.[2] The Master said, You are doing an ill turn to another man's son. Tzu-lu said, What he will take charge of at Pi will be the peasants and the Holy Ground and Millet.[3] Surely 'learning consists in other things besides reading books'.[4] The Master said, It is remarks of that kind that make me hate glib people.[5]

25 Once when Tzu-lu, Tsêng Hsi, Jan Ch'iu and Kung-hsi Hua were seated in attendance upon the Master, he said, You consider me as a somewhat older man than yourselves. Forget for a moment that I am so. At present you are out of office and feel that your merits are not recognised. Now supposing someone were to recognise your merits, what employment would you choose? Tzu-lu promptly and confidently replied, Give me a country of a thousand war-chariots, hemmed in by powerful enemies, or even invaded by hostile armies, with drought and famine to boot; in the space of three years I could endow the people with courage and teach them in what direction[6] right conduct lies.

1   Brother of the head of the Chi Family.
2   See VI, 7.
3   See additional notes.
4   In which the 'stupid' (see XI, 17) Ch'ai was not proficient.
5   The pertness of Tzu-lu's remark consists of the fact that he throws in the Master's teeth a favourite Confucian maxim. cf. I, 14 and Tzu-hsia's saying, I, 7.
6   For *fang* (direction), cf. VI, 28. Courage, it will be remembered, is the lowest of the three virtues. Next comes wisdom; next Goodness.

Our Master smiled at him. What about you, Ch'iu? he said. Ch'iu replied saying, Give me a domain of sixty to seventy or say fifty to sixty (leagues), and in the space of three years I could bring it about that the common people should lack for nothing. But as to rites and music,[1] I should have to leave them to a real gentleman.

What about you, Ch'ih?

(Kung-hsi Hua) answered saying, I do not say I could do this; but I should like at any rate to be trained for it. In ceremonies at the Ancestral Temple or at a conference or general gathering[2] of the feudal princes I should like, clad in the Straight Gown and Emblematic Cap, to play the part of junior assistant.

Tien,[3] what about you?

The notes of the zithern he was softly fingering died away; he put it down, rose and replied saying, I fear my words will not be so well chosen as those of the other three.[4] The Master said, What harm is there in that? All that matters is that each should name his desire.

Tsêng Hsi said, At the end of spring, when the making of the Spring Clothes[5] has been completed, to go with five times six newly-capped youths and six times seven uncapped boys, perform the lustration in the river I, take the air[6] at the Rain Dance altars, and then go home singing. The Master heaved a deep sigh and said, I am with Tien.

When the three others went away, Tsêng Hsi remained behind and said, What about the sayings of those three people?

1 Which are the perquisites of the upper classes as opposed to the common people.

2 Scrupulously defined as 'Audiences' by the later ritualists, because in theory they were presided over by the Son of Heaven (the king of Chou).

3 i.e. Tsêng Hsi; he was the father of Master Tsêng.

4 Or 'I fear my choice will seem inferior to that of . . . '

5 A technical name for the clothes worn at the ceremony?

6 cf. *Mencius*, II, B, 2, where *fêng* means 'expose oneself to the wind'. Freak interpretations such as 'scatter', 'sing', 'sacrifice to the wind' are merely instances of wasted ingenuity.

The Master said, After all, it was agreed that each should tell his wish; and that is just what they did.

Tsêng said, Why did you smile at Yu?

The Master said, 'Because it is upon observance of ritual that the governance of a State depends; and his words were lacking in the virtue of cession.[1] That is why I smiled at him.'

'I suppose you were contrasting him with Ch'iu, who (by domain) certainly did not mean kingdom?'

'Where have you ever seen "a domain of sixty to seventy or fifty to sixty leagues" that was not a kingdom?'

'I suppose, then, you were contrasting him with Ch'ih, who was certainly not asking for a kingdom.'

'The business of the Ancestral Temple and such things as conferences and general gatherings can only be undertaken by feudal princes. But if Ch'ih were taking a minor part, what prince is there who is capable of playing a major one?[2]

1   *Jang*: giving up, ceding to others.
2   i.e. it is impossible to conceive of Kung-hsi Hua functioning on such an occasion except as the ruler of a Kingdom; so that, in effect, all three were asking for kingdoms.

BOOK TWELVE

1   Yen Hui asked about Goodness. The Master said, 'He who can himself submit to ritual is Good.'[1] If (a ruler) could for one day 'himself submit to ritual', everyone under Heaven would respond to his Goodness. For Goodness is something that must have its source in the ruler himself; it cannot be got from others.

Yen Hui said, I beg to ask for the more detailed items of this (submission to ritual). The Master said, To look at nothing in defiance of ritual, to listen to nothing in defiance of ritual, to speak of nothing in defiance of ritual, never to stir hand or foot in defiance of ritual. Yen Hui said, I know that I am not clever; but this is a saying that, with your permission, I shall try to put into practice.[2]

2   Jan Jung asked about Goodness.[3] The Master said, Behave when away from home[4] as though you were in the presence of an important guest. Deal with the common people as though you were officiating at an important sacrifice. Do not do to others what you would not like yourself. Then there will be no feelings of opposition to you, whether it is the affairs of a State that you are handling or the affairs of a Family.[5]

---

1   In the *Tso Chuan* (Chao Kung, 12th year) Confucius is made to quote this as a saying from 'an old record'. The commentators, not understanding the archaic use of *k'o* (able to) turned *k'o chi* into 'self-conquest', an error fruitful in edification.

2   A formula of thanks for instruction; cf. *Mencius*, I, A, 7.

3   i.e. ruling by Goodness, not by force.

4   i.e. in handling public affairs.

5   A ruling clan, such as that of the Chi in Lu.

Jan Yung said, I know that I am not clever; but this is a saying that, with your permission, I shall try to put into practice.

3 Ssu-ma Niu[1] asked about Goodness. The Master said, The Good (*jen*) man is chary (*jen*) of speech. Ssu-ma Niu said, So that is what is meant by Goodness — to be chary of speech? The Master said, Seeing that the doing of it is so difficult, how can one be otherwise than chary of talking about it?[2]

4 Ssu-ma Niu asked about the meaning of the term Gentleman. The Master said, The Gentleman neither grieves nor fears. Ssu-ma Niu said, So that is what is meant by being a gentleman neither to grieve nor to fear? The Master said, On looking within himself he finds no taint; so why should he either grieve or fear?

5 Ssu-ma Niu grieved, saying, Everyone else has brothers; I alone have none.[3] Tzu-hsia said, I have heard this saying, 'Death and life are the decree of Heaven; wealth and rank depend upon the will of Heaven. If a gentleman attends to business and does not idle away his time, if he behaves with courtesy to others and observes the rules of ritual, then all within the Four Seas[4] are his brothers.' How can any true gentleman grieve that he is without brothers?

6 Tzu-chang asked the meaning of the term 'illumined'. The Master said, He who is influenced neither by the soaking in of slander nor by the assault of denunciation may indeed be called illumined.[5] He who is influenced neither by the soaking in of

1 A native of Sung; brother of Huan T'ui, VII, 22.
2 Here again Confucius is evasive about the meaning of Goodness. He first puns on *jen*, 'chary', and *jen*, 'goodness'; and then in his second reply answers as though his first reply had meant 'Goodness is a thing one ought to be chary of talking about.' The implication is that the questioner had not yet reached a stage at which the mysteries of *jen* could be revealed to him.
3 This may merely mean that his brother Huan T'ui, being an enemy of Confucius, could no longer be regarded by Niu as a brother. When Niu died in 481 BC he left behind him at least three brothers.
4 That bound the universe.
5 cf. the section on posthumous titles in the *I Chou Shu*: 'He whom neither slander nor denunciation can influence is called clear-sighted', i.e. in his choice of subordinates.

slander nor by the assault of denunciation may indeed be called 'aloof'.

7 Tzu-kung asked about government. The Master'said, Sufficient food, sufficient weapons, and the confidence of the common people. Tzu-kung said, Suppose you had no choice but to dispense with one of these three, which would you forgo? The Master said, Weapons. Tzu-kung said, Suppose you were forced to dispense with one of the two that were left, which would you forgo? The Master said, Food. For from of old death has been the lot of all men; but a people that no longer trusts its rulers is lost indeed.

8 Chi Tzu-ch'êng[1] said, A gentleman is a gentleman in virtue of the stuff he is made of. Culture cannot make gentlemen. Tzu-kung said, I am sorry, Sir, that you should have said that. For the saying goes that 'when a gentleman has spoken, a team of four horses cannot overtake his words'.[2]

Culture is just as important as inborn qualities; and inborn qualities, no less important than culture. Remove the hairs from the skin of a tiger or panther, and what is left looks just like the hairless hide of a dog or sheep.[3]

9 Duke Ai enquired of Master Yu, saying, It is a year of dearth, and the State has not enough for its needs. What am I to do? Master Yu replied, saying, Have you not got your tithes? The Duke said, Even with two-tenths instead of one, I still should not have enough. What is the use of talking to me about tithes? Master Yu said, When the Hundred Families[4] enjoy plenty, the prince necessarily shares in that plenty. But when the Hundred Families

---

1 A statesman of Wei.

2 Common people can say what they like, and no harm is done. But a person in your position will at once be quoted as an authority. I read a full stop after *shuo*.

3 The man of good birth is potentially capable of 'patterning his coat' with culture, and thus distinguishing himself from the common herd. But good birth alone, though essential as a basis for culture, is not enough to make a gentleman in the Confucian sense.

4 All the people.

have not enough for their needs, the prince cannot expect to have enough for his needs.

10 Tzu-chang asked what was meant by 'piling up moral force'[1] and 'deciding when in two minds'.[2] The Master said, 'by piling up moral force' is meant taking loyalty and good faith as one's guiding principles, and migrating to places where right prevails.[3] Again, to love a thing means wanting it to live, to hate a thing means wanting it to perish. But suppose I want something to live and at the same time want it to perish; that is 'being in two minds'.

> Not for her wealth, oh no!
> But merely for a change.[4]

11 Duke Ching of Ch'i[5] asked Master K'ung about government. Master K'ung replied saying, Let the prince be a prince, the minister a minister, the father a father and the son a son. The

---

1 No wonder Tzu-chang asked this question; for *ch'ung te* (a very common expression in old texts) sometimes (e.g. *Hsi Tz'u,* I, 7; *Tso Chuan,* Hsi Kung, 7th year) means 'to pile up *te*', sometimes (e.g. *Tso Chuan,* Wên Kung, 2nd year), 'to do honour to, exalt possessors of *te*'.

2 The two phrases in inverted commas rhyme, and no doubt Tzu-chang is asking for an explanation of a particular passage in an ancient rhymed text.

3 'If right prevails in a country, then serve it; if right does not prevail, then seek service elsewhere.'

4 Couplet from *Song* 105, 3, in which a lady says: I came all this long way to marry you, and you do not give me enough to eat. I shall go back to my country and home. Your thoughts are occupied with a new mate. If it is true that it is not because of her riches, then it is simply for the sake of a change. The last phrase (only for a change) is susceptible of other interpretations. But it is clearly thus that Confucius understands it, and he uses this story of a man who got a wife from a far country, and then promptly neglected her in favour of someone taken up 'simply for a change', as an example of 'being in two minds', 'not knowing one's own mind'.

5 Died 490 BC. The last of a long line of powerful and successful dukes. The closing years of his reign were clouded by the intrigues of the Ch'ên Family, which menaced the security of the dynasty (the prince

Duke said, How true! For indeed when the prince is not a prince, the minister not a minister, the father not a father, the son not a son, one may have a dish of millet in front of one and yet not know if one will live to eat it.[1]

12 The Master said, Talk about 'deciding a lawsuit with half a word' – Yu is the man for that. Tzu-lu never slept over a promise.[2]

13 The Master said, I could try a civil suit as well as anyone. But better still to bring it about that there were no civil suits![3]

14 Tzu-chang asked about public business. The Master said, Ponder over it untiringly at home; carry it out loyally when the time comes. (Literally, 'Home it untiringly, carry it out loyally.')

15 Repetition of VI, 25.

16 The Master said, The gentleman calls attention to the good points in others; he does not call attention to their defects. The small man does just the reverse of this.

17 Chi K'ang-tzu asked Master K'ung about the art of ruling. Master K'ung said, Ruling (chêng) is straightening (chêng). If you lead along a straight way, who will dare go by a crooked one?

---

was no longer a prince; ministers, i.e. the leaders of the Ch'ên faction, were no longer content to be ministers); and by succession-squabbles among his sons (the father no longer had the authority of a father; the sons were not content to be sons).

1 Figure of speech denoting utter insecurity. Legend makes Duke Ching haunted by the fear of death. cf. *Lieh Tzu*, VI, end. Advice very like that which Confucius gives here was given to Duke Ching's ancestor Duke Huan by Kuan Chung. See *Kuo Yü*, ch. VI, last fol., and *Han Shih Wai Chuan*, X, 9.

2 'He never agreed to do anything that could not be done till next day; for during the night circumstances might alter and prevent him from carrying out his word.' Such is the interpretation of the early commentators. Chu Hsi takes it in the sense of 'never putting off till the morrow'. cf. *Shang Tzu's Su Chih*, 'dilatory government'.

3 cf. *Ta Hsüeh* (*Great Learning*), Commentary, Para. 4.

18 Chi K'ang-tzu was troubled by burglars. He asked Master K'ung what he should do. Master K'ung replied saying, If only you were free from desire, they would not steal even if you paid them to.[1]

19 Chi K'ang-tzu asked Master K'ung about government, saying, Suppose I were to slay those who have not the Way in order to help on those who have the Way, what would you think of it? Master K'ung replied saying, You are there to rule, not to slay. If you desire what is good, the people will at once be good. The essence of the gentleman is that of wind; the essence of small people is that of grass. And when a wind passes over the grass, it cannot choose but bend.[2]

20 Tzu-chang asked what a knight must be like if he is to be called 'influential'.[3] The Master said, That depends on what you mean by 'influential'. Tzu-chang replied saying, If employed by the State, certain to win fame, if employed by a Ruling Family, certain to win fame. The Master said, That describes being famous; it does not describe being influential. In order to be influential a man must be by nature straightforward and a lover of right. He must examine men's words and observe their expressions, and bear in mind the necessity of deferring to others.[4] Such a one, whether employed by the State or by a Ruling Family, will certainly be 'influential'; whereas the man who wins fame may merely have obtained, by his outward airs, a reputation for Goodness which his conduct quite belies. Anyone who makes his claims with sufficient self-assurance is certain to win fame in a State, certain to win fame in a Family.

21 Once when Fan Ch'ih was taking a walk with the Master under the trees at the Rain Dance altars, he said, May I venture to ask about 'piling up moral force', 'repairing shortcomings' and

---

1 This is a rhetorical way of saying that if K'ang-tzu did not accumulate valuables, he would not be robbed. But coupled with this meaning is the suggestion that the ruler's moral force operates directly on the people, as a magic, not merely as an example.

2 cf. *Mencius*, III, A, 2.

3 *Ta*, able to turn his *te* to account. See VI, 6.

4 See additional notes.

'deciding when in two minds'?[1] The Master said, An excellent question. 'The work first; the reward afterwards'; is not that piling up moral force? 'Attack the evil that is within yourself; do not attack the evil that is in others.' Is not this 'repairing shortcomings'?

> 'Because of a morning's blind rage
> To forget one's own safety
> And even endanger one's kith and kin'[2]

is that not a case of 'divided mind'?

22 Fan Ch'ih asked about the Good (ruler). The Master said, He loves men. He asked about the wise (ruler). The Master said, He knows men. Fan Ch'ih did not quite understand.[3] The Master said, By raising the straight and putting them on top of the crooked, he can make the crooked straight.[4] Fan Ch'ih withdrew, and meeting Tzu-hsia said to him, Just now I was with the Master and asked him about the wise (ruler). He said, By raising the straight and putting them on top of the crooked he can make the crooked straight. What did he mean?

Tzu-hsia said, Oh, what a wealth of instruction is in those words! When Shun had all that is under Heaven, choosing from among the multitude he raised up Kao Yao,[5] and straightway Wickedness disappeared. When T'ang had all that is under Heaven, choosing from among the multitude he raised up I Yin;[6] and straightway Wickedness disappeared.

23 Tzu-kung asked about friends. The Master said, inform them loyally and guide them discreetly. If that fails, then desist. Do not court humiliation.

24 Master Tsêng said, The gentleman by his culture collects friends about him, and through these friends promotes Goodness.

1   See above, para. 10. Here all three phrases rhyme; the phrases supplied by Confucius also rhyme, and are presumably quotations from a didactic poem.

2   A rhyming triplet. Not knowing the full context either of the poem which the disciple quotes or of the one which Confucius utilises in his reply, we cannot hope to understand the exact force of this passage.

3   This applies only to the second answer.   4   See above, II, 19.

5   See *The Book of Songs*, p. 268.   6   See *The Book of Songs*, p. 278.

BOOK THIRTEEN

1 Tzu-lu asked about government. The Master said, Lead them; encourage them! Tzu-lu asked for a further maxim. The Master said, Untiringly.

2 Jan Yung, having become steward of the Chi Family, asked about government. The Master said, Get as much as possible done first by your subordinates.[1] Pardon small offences. Promote men of superior capacity. Jan Yung said, How does one know a man of superior capacity, in order to promote him? The Master said, Promote those you know, and those whom you do not know other people will certainly not neglect.[2]

3 Tzu-lu said, If the prince of Wei were waiting for you to come and administer his country for him, what would be your first measure? The Master said, It would certainly be to correct language. Tzu-lu said, Can I have heard you aright? Surely what you say has nothing to do with the matter. Why should language be corrected? The Master said, Yu! How boorish you are! A gentleman, when things he does not understand are mentioned, should maintain an attitude of reserve. If language is incorrect, then what is said does not concord with what was meant; and if what is said does not concord with what was meant, what is to be done cannot be effected. If what is to be done cannot be effected,[3] then rites and music will not flourish. If rites and music

---

1 So that your time may not be taken up with petty preliminaries.
2 i.e. will certainly bring to your notice.
3 The 'chain argument' clanks rather heavily in English; but it is essential to preserve the form of the original.

do not flourish, then mutilations and lesser punishments will go astray. And if mutilations and lesser punishments go astray, then the people have nowhere to put hand or foot.

Therefore the gentleman uses only such language as is proper for speech, and only speaks of what it would be proper to carry into effect. The gentleman, in what he says, leaves nothing to mere chance.[1]

4   Fan Ch'ih asked the Master to teach him about farming. The Master said, You had much better consult some old farmer. He asked to be taught about gardening. The Master said, You had much better go to some old vegetable-gardener. When Fan Ch'ih had gone out, the Master said, Fan is no gentleman! If those above them love ritual, then among the common people none will dare to be disrespectful. If those above them love right, then among the common people none will dare to be disobedient. If those above them love good faith, then among the common people none will dare depart from the facts.[2] If a gentleman is like that, the common people will flock to him from all sides with their babies strapped to their backs. What need has he to practise farming?[3]

5   The Master said, A man may be able to recite the three hundred Songs; but, if when given a post in the government, he cannot turn his merits to account, or when sent on a mission to far parts he cannot answer particular questions,[4] however extensive his knowledge may be, of what use is it to him?

1   The whole of this highly elaborate, literary paragraph bears the stamp of comparatively late date. The links in chain-arguments of this kind are always rhetorical rather than logical; and it would be a waste of time to seek for a causal sequence. Later Confucian literature supplies many examples of such rhetorical 'chains'. For kou (chance), see additional notes.

2   Bear false witness in lawsuits.

3   See additional notes.

4   Besides delivering his message, he must be able to give an answer of his own to particular enquiries relative to this message.

6 The Master said, If the ruler himself is upright all will go well even though he does not give orders. But if he himself is not upright, even though he gives orders, they will not be obeyed.

7 The Master said, In their politics Lu and Wei are still brothers.[1]

8 The Master said of the Wei grandee Ching,[2] He dwelt as a man should dwell in his house. When things began to prosper with him, he said, 'Now they[3] will begin to be a little more suitable.' When he was better off still, he said, 'Now they will be fairly complete.' When he was really rich, he said, 'Now I shall be able to make them quite beautiful.'

9 When the Master was going to Wei, Jan Ch'iu drove him. The Master said, What a dense population! Jan Ch'iu said, When the people have multiplied, what next should be done for them? The Master said, Enrich them. Jan Ch'iu said, When one has enriched them, what next should be done for them? The Master said, Instruct them.

10 The Master said, If only someone were to make use of me, even for a single year, I could do a great deal; and in three years I could finish off the whole work.

11 The Master said, 'Only if the right sort of people had charge of a country for a hundred years would it become really possible to stop cruelty and do away with slaughter.' How true the saying is!

12 The Master said, If a Kingly Man were to arise, within a single generation Goodness would prevail.

---

1 On the rise of the Chou dynasty to power, Lu was given to the fourth and Wei to the seventh son of King Wên. The saying expresses, one may suppose, the disillusionment of Confucius on finding that things in Wei were no better than in Lu. In early times, however, it was understood as a commendation of Wei.

2 Flourished about 558 BC.

3 My household rites.

13 The Master said, Once a man has contrived to put himself aright, he will find no difficulty at all in filling any government post. But if he cannot put himself aright, how can he hope to succeed in putting others right? [1]

14 Once when Master Jan came back from Court,[2] the Master said, Why are you so late? He replied, saying, There were affairs of State. The Master said, You must mean private business. If there had been affairs of State, although I am not used,[3] I too should have been bound to hear of them.

15 Duke Ting[4] asked if there were any one phrase that sufficed to save a country. Master K'ung replied saying, No phrase could ever be like that.[5] But here is one that comes near to it. There is a saying among men: 'It is hard to be a prince and not easy to be a minister.' A ruler who really understood that it was 'hard to be a prince' would have come fairly near to saving his country by a single phrase.

Duke Ting said, Is there any one phrase that could ruin a country? Master K'ung said, No phrase could ever be like that. But here is one that comes near to it. There is a saying among men: 'What pleasure is there in being a prince, unless one can say whatever one chooses, and no one dares to disagree?'[6] So long as what he says is good, it is of course good also that he should not be opposed. But if what he says is bad, will it not come very near to his ruining his country by a single phrase?

1   The play on *chêng* 'to straighten, put right' and *chêng* 'to govern' makes this passage impossible to translate satisfactorily.
2   From the Court of the Chi Family, who had usurped the Duke's powers.
3   i.e. have no official post.
4   See above, III, 19.
5   The stop should come after *jo shih*.
6   This saying also occurs in *Han Fei Tzu*, P'ien, 36.

16 The 'Duke' of Shê [1] asked about government.[2] The Master said, When the near approve and the distant approach.

17 When Tzu-hsia was Warden of Chü-fu,[3] he asked for advice about government. The Master said, Do not try to hurry things. Ignore minor considerations. If you hurry things, your personality will not come into play.[4] If you let yourself be distracted by minor considerations, nothing important will ever get finished.

18 The 'Duke' of Shê addressed Master K'ung saying, In my country there was a man called Upright Kung.[5] His father appropriated a sheep, and Kung bore witness against him. Master K'ung said, In my country the upright men are of quite another sort. A father will screen his son, and a son his father – which incidentally[6] does involve a sort of uprightness.

19 Fan Ch'ih asked about Goodness. The Master said, In private life, courteous, in public life, diligent, in relationships, loyal. This is a maxim that no matter where you may be, even amid the barbarians of the east or north, may never be set aside.

20 Tzu-kung asked, What must a man be like in order that he may be called a true knight (of the Way)? The Master said, He who

> In the furtherance of his own interests
> Is held back by scruples,
> Who as an envoy to far lands
> Does not disgrace his prince's commission

may be called a true knight.
 Tzu-kung said, May I venture to ask who would rank next?

---

1 See above VII, 18. cf. *Han Fei Tzu*, P'ien, 38 and *Mo Tzu*, P'ien, 46 (*Kêng Chu*).
2 i.e. about the tokens of good government.
3 A town in Lu.
4 For *ta*, see VI, 6.
5 A legendary paragon of honesty; see *Huai-nan Tzu*, ch. XIII, fol. 6, where he is coupled with Wei-sheng Kao, *Han Fei Tzu*, P'ien, 49, and *Lü Shih Ch'un Ch'iu*, P'ien, 54.
6 For the idiom see II, 18 and VII, 15.

The Master said, He whom his relatives commend for filial piety, his fellow-villagers, for deference to his elders. Tzu-kung said, May I venture to ask who would rank next? The Master said, He who always stands by his word, who undertakes nothing that he does not bring to achievement. Such a one may be in the humblest[1] possible circumstances, but all the same we must give him the next place.

Tzu-kung said, What would you say of those who are now conducting the government? The Master said, Ugh! A set of peck-measures,[2] not worth taking into account.

21 The Master said, If I cannot get men who steer a middle course to associate with, I would far rather have the impetuous and hasty.[3] For the impetuous at any rate assert themselves; and the hasty have this at least to be said for them, that there are things they leave undone.[4]

22 The Master said, The men of the south have a saying, 'Without stability[5] a man will not even make a good *shaman* or witch-doctor.'[6] Well said! Of the maxim: if you do not stabilise an act of *te,* you will get evil by it (instead of good), the Master said, They (i.e. soothsayers) do not simply read the omens.[7]

1 For *k'êng k'êng,* see XIV, 42.
2 'Mere thimblefuls', as we should say.
3 than the timid and conscientious.
4 cf. *Mencius,* VII, B, 37.
5 Play on *hêng* (1) a rite for stabilising, perpetuating the power of good omens and auspicious actions (see additional notes); (2) steadfast, in the moral sense.
6 For '*shaman* or witch-doctor' the *Li Chi* (33, fol. 3) has 'diviner by the yarrow stalks'.
7 To 'read the omens' is the first step in any undertaking. cf. our own word 'inaugurate'. In its moral application Confucius's remark means that it is not enough to embark on the Way; the real test is whether one can continue in it.

23 The Master said, The true gentleman is conciliatory but not accommodating. Common people are accommodating but not conciliatory.[1]

24 Tzu-kung asked, saying, What would you feel about a man who was loved by all his fellow-villagers? The Master said, That is not enough.

What would you feel about a man who was hated by all his fellow-villagers? The Master said, That is not enough. Best of all would be that the good people in his village loved him and the bad hated him.

25 The Master said, The true gentleman is easy to serve, yet difficult to please.[2] For if you try to please him in any manner inconsistent with the Way, he refuses to be pleased; but in using the services of others he only expects of them what they are capable of performing. Common people are difficult to serve, but easy to please. Even though you try to please them in a manner inconsistent with the Way, they will still be pleased; but in using the services of others they expect them (irrespective of their capacities) to do any work that comes along.

26 The Master said, The gentleman is dignified, but never haughty; common people are haughty, but never dignified.

27 The Master said, Imperturbable, resolute, tree-like,[3] slow to speak — such a one is near to Goodness.

28 Tzu-lu asked, What must a man be like, that he may be called a true knight of the Way? The Master said, He must be critical and exacting, but at the same time indulgent. Then he may be called a true knight. Critical and exacting with regard to the conduct of his friends; indulgent towards his brothers.

1 'Accommodating' (*t'ung*) means ready to sacrifice principles to agreement. cf. the common phrase *kou t'ung*, 'to agree somehow or other', i.e. at all costs.

2 cf. *Hsün Tzu*, P'ien, 27, end.

3 Or 'wooden', i.e. simple.

29, 30 The Master said, Only when men of the right sort[1] have instructed a people for seven years ought there to be any talk of engaging them in warfare. The Master said, To lead into battle a people that has not first been instructed is to betray them.[2]

---

1 i.e. followers of the Way. The 'instruction' is, of course, in virtue, not in the use of arms.

2 cf. *Mencius*, VI, B, 8, and *Ku-liang Chuan*, Duke Hsi, 23rd year.

BOOK FOURTEEN

1   Yüan Ssu asked about compunction.[1] The Master said, When a country is ruled according to the Way, (the gentleman) accepts rewards. But when a country is not ruled according to the Way, he shows compunction in regard to rewards.

2   Of the saying 'He upon whom neither love of mastery, vanity, resentment nor covetousness have any hold may be called Good,' the Master said, Such a one has done what is difficult;[2] but whether he should be called Good I do not know.

3   The Master said, The knight of the Way who thinks only of sitting quietly at home is not worthy to be called a knight.

4   The Master said, When the Way prevails in the land, be bold in speech and bold in action. When the Way does not prevail, be bold in action but conciliatory in speech.

5   The Master said, One who has accumulated moral power (te) will certainly also possess eloquence; but he who has eloquence does not necessarily possess moral power. A Good Man will certainly also possess courage; but a brave man is not necessarily Good.

1   With regard to accepting rewards. It will be remembered that it was Yüan Ssu (see above, VI, 3) who was rebuked for refusing a salary. The omission of his surname has led to the supposition that he was the compiler of this chapter.

2   cf. VI, 20.

6   Nan-kung Kuo[1] asked Master K'ung, saying, Yi[2] was a mighty
     archer and Ao shook the boat;[3] yet both of them came to a bad
     end.[4] Whereas Yü and Chi, who devoted themselves to agriculture,
     came into possession of all that is under Heaven.[5]

     At the time our Master made no reply, but when Nan-kung
     had withdrawn he said, He is a true gentleman indeed, is that
     man! He has a right appraisal of 'virtue's power' (te),[6] has that man!

7   The Master said, It is possible to be a true gentleman and yet lack
     Goodness. But there has never yet existed a Good man who was
     not a gentleman.

8   The Master said, How can he be said truly to love,[7] who exacts no
     effort from the objects of his love? How can he be said to be truly
     loyal, who refrains from admonishing the object of his loyalty?

9   The Master said, When a ducal mandate was being prepared[8] P'i
     Ch'ên[9] first made a rough draft, Shih Shu[10] checked and revised
     it, Tzu-yü[11] the Receiver of Envoys amended and embellished
     it; Tzu-ch'an[12] of Tung-li gave it amplitude and colour.

1   Son of Mêng I Tzu; see II, 5.
2   A legendary hero. His name is cognate to the word for rainbow.
3   Shook his enemies out of it, at the great battle in which he destroyed
     the Shên-hsün clan.
4   Yi was slain by his minister Shu (or Cho) of Han. Shu's son Ao was in
     turn slain by Shao K'ang. For the legend, see *Tso Chuan*, Hsiang Kung,
     4th year, and the *T'ien Wên*, verse 90.
5   For Great Yü drained the land and so made it suitable for agriculture.
     Hou Chi, from whom the Chou people were descended, was (as his
     name implies; *chi* = millet) the patron deity of agriculture.
6   As opposed to physical strength such as that displayed by Yi and Ao.
7   As a father loves a son or a prince his people.
8   In the State of Chêng.
9   Flourished in the middle of the sixth century BC.
10   Grandson of Duke Mou of Chêng; died in 506 BC.
11   Perhaps Yü Chieh, great-grandson of Duke Mou. He is the 'Receiver
     of Envoys Tzu-yü of Chêng' mentioned in *Tso Chuan*, Hsiang kung,
     29th year.
12   See V, 15 and note.

10, 11 Someone asked about Tzu-ch'an. The Master said, A kindly[1] man! Asked about Tzu-hsi[2] he said, That man! That man! Asked about Kuan Chung[3] he said, This is the sort of man he was: he could seize the fief of Pien with its three hundred villages[4] from its owner, the head of the Po Family; yet Po, though he 'lived on coarse food'[5] to the end of his days, never uttered a single word of resentment.[6] The Master said, To be poor and not resent it[7] is far harder than to be rich, yet not presumptuous.[8]

12 The Master said, Mêng Kung Ch'o would have done well enough as Comptroller of the Chao or Wei families; but he was not fit to be a State minister even in T'êng or Hsüeh.[9]

---

1   The word is often used in a bad sense. Kindliness is often a feeble amends for neglect of duty. Thus Tzu-ch'an took people across the rivers in his own carriage; but he ought to have mended the bridges. *Mencius,* IV, B, 2.

2   A famous minister of the Ch'u State; assassinated in 479 BC. According to the accounts of him in the *Tso Chuan* he did and said much of which Confucius would certainly have approved. The exclamation with which his name is here received is, however, certainly one of disapprobation. The story that he prejudiced his prince against Confucius was probably merely invented to explain this passage.

3   See III, 22.

4   cf. *Hsün Tzu,* P'ien, 7, fol. 1.

5   A stock expression, merely meaning 'in humble circumstances'.

6   So great was Kuan Chung's prestige. This is the tenor of many stories about Kuan Chung. He struck with an arrow the man who was afterwards to become Duke Huan of Ch'i; yet the Duke forgave him and made him Prime Minister. He broke all the sumptuary laws; yet it never occurred to the people of Ch'i to regard him as 'presumptuous'.

7   As the head of the Po Family managed to do.

8   In which respect, according to Confucius's view (see III, 22), Kuan Chung signally failed.

9   Let alone in a great State like Lu. Mêng Kung Ch'o was a Lu politician who flourished about 548 BC. The Chao and Wei were noble families in Chin.

13   Tzu-lu asked what was meant by 'the perfect man'. The Master
     said, If anyone had the wisdom of Tsang Wu Chung,[1] the
     uncovetousness of Mêng Kung Ch'o, the valour of Chuang Tzu
     of P'ien[2] and the dexterity of Jan Ch'iu,[3] and had graced these
     virtues by the cultivation of ritual and music, then indeed I think
     we might call him 'a perfect man'.

        He said, But perhaps today we need not ask all this of the
     perfect man. One who, when he sees a chance of gain, stops to
     think whether to pursue it would be right; when he sees that (his
     prince) is in danger, is ready to lay down his life; when the
     fulfilment of an old promise is exacted, stands by what he said
     long ago – him indeed I think we might call 'a perfect man'.

14   The Master asked Kung-ming Chia[4] about Kung-shu Wên-tzu,[5]
     saying, Is it a fact that your master neither 'spoke nor laughed nor
     took'? Kung-ming Chia replied saying, The people who told
     you this were exaggerating. My master never spoke till the time
     came to do so; with the result that people never felt that they had
     had too much of his talk. He never laughed unless he was
     delighted; so people never felt they had had too much of his
     laughter. He never took[6] unless it was right to do so, so that
     people never felt he had done too much taking. The Master said,
     Was that so? Can that really have been so?

1   Middle of the sixth century; grandson of Tsang Wên Chung, V, 17.
2   The paragon of legendary prowess. See *Hsin Hsü*, VIII.
3   It is very odd to find the disciple Jan Ch'iu ranged alongside of
    worthies who belonged to a past generation and contrasted with the
    men of 'to-day'. I suspect that some earlier member of the Jan family is
    intended, perhaps Jan Shu, whose marksmanship at a battle between
    Ch'i and Lu (516 BC) is mentioned in the *Tso Chuan*. The familiar
    name of Jan Ch'iu might then easily have been substituted by a scribe.
4   Presumably a retainer of Kung-shu Wên-tzu.
5   Spoken of as 'very aged' in 504 BC, and apparently dead in 497 BC, the
    year (according to the traditional chronology) of Confucius's first visit
    to Wei, Wen-tzu's native place. See *Tso Chuan*, Ting Kung, 6th year
    and 13th year.
6   Took rewards.

15 The Master said, Tsang Wu Chung occupied the fief of Fang and then demanded from (the Duke of) Lu that (his brother) Wei should be allowed to take the fief over from him. It is said that he applied no pressure upon his prince; but I do not believe it.[1]

16 The Master said, Duke Wên of Chin could rise to an emergency, but failed to carry out the plain dictates of ritual. Duke Huan of Ch'i carried out the dictates of ritual, but failed when it came to an emergency.[2]

17 Tzu-lu said, When Duke Huan put to death (his brother) Prince Chiu, Shao Hu gave his life in an attempt to save the prince; but Kuan Chung did not.[3] Must one not say that he fell short of Goodness? The Master said, That Duke Huan was able to convene the rulers of all the States without resorting to the use of his war-chariots was due to Kuan Chung. But as to his[4] Goodness, as to his Goodness!

18 Tzu-kung said, I fear Kuan Chung was not Good. When Duke Huan put to death his brother Prince Chiu, Kuan Chung so far from dying on Chiu's behalf became Duke Huan's Prime Minister. The Master said, Through having Kuan Chung as his Minister Duke Huan became leader of the feudal princes, uniting

---

1 In 550 BC Tsang Wu Chung, accused of plotting a revolt, was obliged to go into exile. On his way he seized the fief of Fang, and then sent word to the Duke offering to proceed into exile and relinquish Fang, on condition that he should be allowed to hand the fief over to his brother Tsang Wei. The request was granted. (*Tso Chuan*, Duke Hsiang, 23rd year.) The later commentators fail to realise that 'Wei' is a proper name and unsuccessfully attempt to turn it into *wei* 'to do'. Translators have followed suit.

2 See additional notes.

3 Both Kuan Chung and Shao Hu were supporting Prince Chiu's claim to the dukedom. Prince Hsiao Po (afterwards to become Duke Huan) murdered his brother Prince Chiu and seized the ducal throne; whereupon Kuan Chung, the great opportunist, transferred his allegiance to the murderer.

4 i.e. Kuan Chung's.

and reducing to good order all that is under Heaven; so that even today the people are benefiting by what he then did for them. Were it not for Kuan Chung we might now be wearing our hair loose and folding our clothes to the left![1] We must not expect from him what ordinary men and women regard as 'true constancy' – to go off and strangle oneself in some ditch or drain, and no one the wiser.

19 Kung-shu Wên-tzu, when summoned to office by the Duke (of Wei), brought with him and presented to the Duke his retainer Chuan,[2] the same Chuan who became a State officer. The Master hearing of it[3] said, With good reason was he accorded the title Wên.[4]

20 The Master referred to Duke Ling of Wei as being no follower of the true Way. K'ang-tzu[5] said, How is it then that he does not come to grief? Master K'ung said, He has Chung-shu Yü[6] to deal with foreign envoys and guests, the priest T'o[7] to regulate the ceremonies in his ancestral temple and Wang-sun Chia[8] to command his armies. Why then should he come to grief?

21 The Master said, Do not be too ready to speak of it,[9] lest the doing of it should prove to be beyond your powers.

1 As the barbarians do. Duke Huan stemmed the great invasion of the Ti tribes.
2 Or Hsien. It is necessary slightly to paraphrase this sentence in order to bring out the meaning with clarity.
3 As a historical event; not at the time when it happened.
4 cf. *I Chou Shu*, 54, fol. 1, 'He who helps commoners to rank and position is called Wên.' So various were Kung-shu Wên-tzu's merits that the business of choosing his posthumous title was unusually difficult. See *Li Chi*, IV, fol. 5.
5 The head of the Chi Family.
6 Known posthumously as K'ung Wên Tzu. See V, 14.
7 See VI, 14.
8 See III, 13.
9 Goodness. cf. XII, 3.

22 When Ch'ên Hêng assassinated Duke Chien of Ch'i, Master K'ung washed his head and limbs,[1] went to Court and informed Duke Ai of Lu, saying, Ch'ên Hêng has slain his prince. I petition that steps should be taken to punish him. The Duke said, You had better inform the Three.[2] Master K'ung said, As I rank next to the Great Officers,[3] I could not do otherwise than lay this information before you. And now your Highness says 'Inform the Three'? He then went to the Three and informed them. They refused his petition. Master K'ung said, As I rank next to the Great Officers, I could not do otherwise than lay this petition before you.

23 Tzu-lu asked him how to serve a prince. The Master said, Never oppose him by subterfuges.[4]

24 The Master said, The gentleman can influence those who are above him; the small man can only influence those who are below him.

25 The Master said, In old days men studied for the sake of self-improvement; nowadays men study in order to impress other people.[5]

26 Ch'ü Po Yü[6] sent a messenger to Master K'ung. Master K'ung bade the man be seated and asked of him saying, What is your master doing? He replied, saying, My master is trying to diminish the number of his failings;[7] but he has not hitherto been successful. When the messenger had gone away, the Master said, What a messenger, what a messenger![8]

1 As became a suppliant. The assassination took place in 481 BC.
2 The heads of the three great families Chi, Shu and Mêng.
3 cf. XI, 7. This anecdote, in a very similar form, occurs in the *Tso Chuan*, Ai, 14th year.
4 But if you have to oppose him, do so openly.
5 cf. *Hsün Tzu*, P'ien, 1.
6 A famous Wei minister. See below, XV, 6.
7 Or 'is trying to lessen his offence'. Chü Po Yü may have promised to get Confucius a post in Wei and failed to do so. The message may mean that he is still trying, but has not yet succeeded arranging anything.
8 This is usually taken as an exclamation of approval. I very much doubt if that is so.

27, 28 When the Master said, He who holds no rank in a State does not discuss its policies,[1] Master Tsêng said, A true gentleman, even in his thoughts, never departs from what is suitable to his rank.[2]

29 The Master said, A gentleman is ashamed to let his words outrun his deeds.

30 The Master said, The Ways of the true gentleman are three. I myself have met with success in none of them. For he that is really Good is never unhappy, he that is really wise is never perplexed, he that is really brave is never afraid. Tzu-kung said, That, Master, is your own Way![3]

31 Tzu-kung was always criticising other people. The Master said, It is fortunate for Ssu that he is so perfect himself as to have time to spare for this. I myself have none.

32 The Master said, (A gentleman) does not grieve that people do not recognise his merits; he grieves at his own incapacities.

33 The Master said, Is it the man who 'does not count beforehand upon the falsity of others nor reckon upon promises not being kept', or he who is conscious beforehand of deceit, that is the true sage?[4]

34 Wei-shêng Mou said to Master K'ung, Ch'iu,[5] what is your object in going round perching now here, now there? Is it not

1 See above, VIII, 14.
2 Tsêng illustrates Confucius's saying by quoting an old maxim, which also figures, in practically identical form, in the first appendix (Hsiang) of the Book of Changes, section 52.
3 Is precisely how you yourself behave. Usually taken as referring to Confucius's disclaimer ('I myself have met with success in none,' etc.) and meaning, 'So you yourself say; (but we know that is only due to your modesty, and do not take your words literally).'
4 See additional notes.
5 Familiar name of Confucius, the form of address is discourteous. It is surmised that Wei-shêng Mou was a recluse.

simply to show off the fact that you are a clever talker? Master K'ung said, I have no desire to be thought a clever talker; but I do not approve of obstinacy.[1]

35 The Master said, The horse Chi[2] was not famed for its strength but for its inner qualities (*te*).

36 Someone said, What about the saying 'Meet resentment with inner power (*te*)'?[3] The Master said, In that case, how is one to meet inner power? Rather, meet resentment with upright dealing and meet inner power with inner power.

37 The Master said, The truth is, no one knows me![4] Tzu-kung said, What is the reason that you are not known? The Master said, I do not 'accuse Heaven, nor do I lay the blame on men'.[5]

But the studies[6] of men here below are felt on high, and perhaps after all I am known; not here, but in Heaven !

38 Kung-po Liao spoke against Tzu-lu to the Chi Family. Tzu-fu Ching-po[7] informed the Master saying, I fear my master's[8] mind has been greatly unsettled by this. But in the case of Kung-po Liao, I believe my influence is still great enough to have his carcase exposed in the market-place. The Master said, If it is the will of Heaven that the Way shall prevail, then the Way will prevail. But if it is the will of Heaven that the Way should perish, then it must needs perish. What can Kung-po Liao do against Heaven's will?

1 It is no use going on and on trying to convert a prince. After a time one must give it up, and try elsewhere.
2 A famous horse of ancient times. A rhymed couplet.
3 The same saying is utilised in the *Tao Tê Ching*, ch. 63. It originally meant 'Let the ruler meet discontent among his subjects with *te* and not with violence.' Confucius here uses it in a much more general sense.
4 No ruler recognises my merits and employs me.
5 'A gentleman neither accuses Heaven nor blames men.' *Mencius*, II, B, 13.
6 The self-training consisting in the study of antiquity.
7 A retainer of the Chi Family, friendly with Tzu-kung.
8 Chi K'ang-tzu's.

39 The Master said, Best of all, to withdraw from one's generation; next to withdraw to another land; next to leave because of a look; next best to leave because of a word.[1]

40 The Master said, The makers[2] were seven . . .

41 Tzu-lu was spending the night at the Stone Gates.[3] The gate-keeper said, Where are you from? Tzu-lu said, From Master K'ung's. The man said, He's the one who 'knows it's no use, but keeps on doing it', is that not so?

42 The Master was playing the stone-chimes, during the time when he was in Wei. A man carrying a basket passed the house where he and his disciples had established themselves. He said, How passionately he beats his chimes! When the tune was over, he said, How petty and small-minded![4] A man whose talents no one recognises has but one course open to him – to mind his own business! 'If the water is deep, use the stepping-stones; if it is shallow, then hold up your skirts.'[5] The Master said, That is indeed[6] an easy way out!

---

1 This continues the theme of the last paragraph. If *Tao* (the Way) does not prevail, it is better to flee altogether from the men of one's generation, rather than to go round 'perching first here, then there' as Confucius himself had unsuccessfully done, or to wait till the expression of the ruler's face betrays that he is meditating some enormity, or worst of all, to wait till his words actually reveal his intention.

2 i. e. inventors, 'culture-heroes', originators of fire, agriculture, metallurgy, boats, carriages, the potter's wheel, the loom. Their names are variously given. It is natural to suppose that the compilers could not agree as to which names Confucius had enumerated, and therefore left the paragraph unfinished.

3 On the frontiers of Lu and Ch'i? Both this and the next paragraph belong to popular legend rather than to the traditions of the school. cf. Book XVIII.

4 cf. XIII, 20. He sees in Confucius's passionate playing an expression of discontent at his failure to get office.

5 In *Song* 54. The meaning here is, 'Take the world as you find it.'

6 *Kuo* here means 'en effet', not 'effective', 'resolute'. cf. *Mencius*, IV, B, 32.

43 Tzu-chang said, The Books[1] say, 'When Kao Tsung was in the Shed of Constancy,[2] he did not speak for three years.' What does this mean? The Master said, Not Kao Tsung in particular. All the men of old did this. Whenever a prince died, the ministers (of the last prince) all continued in their offices, taking their orders from the Prime Minister;[3] and this lasted for three years.

44 The Master said, So long as the ruler loves ritual,[4] the people will be easy to handle.

45 Tzu-lu asked about the qualities of a true gentleman. The Master said, He cultivates in himself the capacity to be diligent in his tasks. Tzu-lu said, Can he not go further than that? The Master said, He cultivates in himself the capacity to ease the lot of other people.[5] Tzu-lu said, Can he not go further than that? The Master said, He cultivates in himself the capacity to ease the lot of the whole populace. If he can do that, could even Yao or Shun find cause to criticise him?[6]

46 Yüan Jang sat waiting for the Master in a sprawling position.[7] The Master said, Those who when young show no respect to their elders achieve nothing worth mentioning when they grow up. And merely to live on, getting older and older, is to be a useless pest.[8]

And he struck him across the shins with his stick.

1 See *Shu Ching*, Wu Yi. cf. *Kuo Yü*, 20, fol. 2.
2 i.e. in mourning for his father. The *liang-an* was a penthouse set up for the habitation of a mourner against the wall of a tomb. Kao Tsung's traditional date is 1324–1266 BC.
3 cf. *Mencius*, III, A, 2.
4 i.e. carries on immemorial usages and customs.
5 Other gentlemen.
6 cf. VI, 28.
7 Whereas he ought to have been standing when his teacher arrived and only to have sat down when told to do so.
8 This paragraph is usually translated in a way which makes it appear that Yüan Jang was an old man, whom Confucius brutally reproaches with 'being old and not dying'. It is, on the contrary, clear that he was a young man, like the boy of the next paragraph.

47 A boy from the village of Ch'uëh used to come with messages.
Someone asked about him, saying, Is he improving himself?[1]
The Master said, Judging by the way he sits in grown-up people's
places and walks alongside of people older than himself, I should
say he was bent upon getting on quickly rather than upon
improving himself.

---

1   i.e. taking advantage of his visits to the house of Confucius.

BOOK FIFTEEN

1   Duke Ling of Wei asked Master K'ung about the marshalling of troops. Master K'ung replied saying, About the ordering of ritual vessels I have some knowledge; but warfare is a thing I have never studied. Next day he resumed his travels.[1] In Ch'ên supplies fell short and his followers became so weak that they could not drag themselves on to their feet. Tzu-lu came to the Master and said indignantly, Is it right that even gentlemen should be reduced to such straits? The Master said, A gentleman can withstand hardships; it is only the small man who, when submitted to them, is swept off his feet.[2]

2   The Master said, Ssu,[3] I believe you look upon me as one whose aim is simply to learn and retain in mind as many things as possible. He replied, That is what I thought. Is it not so? The Master said, No; I have one (thread) upon which I string them all.[4]

3   The Master said, Yu,[5] those who understand moral force (te) are few.

---

1   There is a similar story in the *Tso Chuan*, Ai Kung, 11th year.
2   As though by a flood.
3   Familiar name of Tzu-kung.
4   cf. IV, 15.
5   Familiar name of Tzu-lu.

4   The Master said, Among those that 'ruled by inactivity'[1] surely Shun may be counted. For what action did he take? He merely placed himself gravely and reverently with his face due south;[2] that was all.

5   Tzu-chang asked about getting on with people. The Master said, Be loyal and true to your every word, serious and careful in all you do; and you will get on well enough, even though you find yourself among barbarians. But if you are disloyal and untrustworthy in your speech, frivolous and careless in your acts, even though you are among your own neighbours, how can you hope to get on well? When standing,[3] see these principles ranged before you; in your carriage, see them resting on the yoke. Then you may be sure that you will get on. Tzu-chang accordingly inscribed the maxim upon his sash.

6   The Master said, Straight and upright indeed was the recorder Yü![4] When the Way prevailed in the land he was (straight) as an arrow; when the Way ceased to prevail, he was (straight) as an arrow. A gentleman indeed is Ch'ü Po Yü.[5] When the Way prevailed in his land, he served the State; but when the Way ceased to prevail, he knew how to 'wrap it[6] up and hide it in the folds of his dress'.

1   *Wu-wei*, the phrase applied by the Taoists to the immobility of self-hypnosis.
2   The position of the ruler. Shun was a Divine Sage (*shêng*) whose *te* was so great that it sufficed to guide and transform the people.
3   In your place at Court.
4   Having failed to persuade Duke Ling of Wei to use the services of Ch'ü Po Yü, the recorder Yü gave directions that when he (the recorder) died his body should not receive the honours due to a minister, as a posthumous protest against the Duke Ling's offences. The story is told in *Han Shih Wai Chuan*, 7, and many other places.
5   Ch'ü Po Yü left Wei owing to the tyrannical conduct of Duke Hsien in 559 BC. No tense is expressed in the first clause. I say 'is' because in XIV, 26, Ch'ü Po Yü appears to be still alive. It is, however, not very probable that he was, as legend asserts, still alive when Confucius visited Wei in 495 BC
6   His jewel; i.e. his talents.

7 The Master said, Not to talk to[1] one who could be talked to, is to waste a man. To talk to those who cannot be talked to, is to waste one's words. 'He who is truly wise never wastes a man';[2] but on the other hand, he never wastes his words.

8 The Master said, Neither the knight who has truly the heart of a knight nor the man of good stock who has the qualities that belong to good stock[3] will ever seek life at the expense of Goodness; and it may be that he has to give his life in order to achieve Goodness.

9 Tzu-kung asked how to become Good. The Master said, A craftsman, if he means to do good work, must first sharpen his tools. In whatever State you dwell

Take service with such of its officers as are worthy,
Make friends with such of its knights as are Good.

10 Yen Hui asked about the making of a State. The Master said, One would go by the seasons of Hsia;[4] as State-coach for the ruler one would use that of Yin,[5] and as head-gear of ceremony wear the Chou hat.[6] For music one would take as model the Succession Dance,[7] and would do away altogether with the tunes of Chêng;[8] one would also keep clever talkers at a distance. For the tunes of Chêng are licentious and clever talkers are dangerous.

1 About the Way. cf. VII, 28.
2 I suspect that this is a proverbial saying.
3 The written forms of *chih* and *jen* are here half-punningly insisted upon.
4 It was believed that in the Hsia dynasty the year began in the spring.
5 Which were less ornate than those of Chou, say the commentators. But this is a mere guess. *Han Fei Tzu*, P'ien, 10, says that the Yin invented state coaches.
6 Which had some resemblance to our scholastic mortar-board.
7 See above, III, 25 and VII, 13.
8 The words to these tunes are in the seventh book of the *Songs*. But it was probably to the character of the music not to that of the words that Confucius objected. See additional notes.

11 The Master said, He who will not worry about what is far off will soon find something worse[1] than worry close at hand.

12 The Master said, In vain have I looked for one whose desire to build up his moral power was as strong as sexual desire.[2]

13 The Master said, Surely one would not be wrong in calling Tsang Wên Chung[3] a stealer of other men's ranks? He knew that Liu-hsia Hui was the best man for the post, yet would not have him as his colleague.[4]

14 The Master said, To demand much from oneself and little from others is the way (for a ruler) to banish discontent.

15 The Master said, If a man does not continually ask himself 'What am I to do about this, what am I to do about this?' there is no possibility of my doing anything about him.

16 The Master said, Those who are capable of spending a whole day together without ever once discussing questions of right or wrong, but who content themselves[5] with performing petty acts of clemency, are indeed difficult.[6]

17 The Master said, The gentleman who takes the right as his material to work upon and ritual as the guide in putting what is right into practice, who is modest in setting out his projects and faithful in carrying them to their conclusion, he indeed is a true gentleman.

18 The Master said, A gentleman is distressed by his own lack of capacity; he is never distressed at the failure of others to recognise his merits.

1 *Yu* is a much stronger word than *lü*.
2 cf. IX, 17.
3 See V, 17.
4 'Degraded him', says the *Tso Chuan*, Wên Kung, 2nd year. For Liu-hsia Hui, see below, XVIII, 2.
5 'Satisfy their consciences', as we should say.
6 To lead into the Way.

19 The Master said, A gentleman has reason to be distressed if he ends his days without making a reputation for himself.[1]

20 The Master said, The demands that a gentleman makes are upon himself; those that a small man makes are upon others.[2]

21 The Master said, A gentleman is proud, but not quarrelsome, allies himself with individuals, but not with parties.

22 The Master said, A gentleman does not

> Accept men because of what they say,
> Nor reject sayings, because the speaker is what he is.

23 Tzu-kung asked saying, Is there any single saying that one can act upon all day and every day?[3] The Master said, Perhaps the saying about consideration:[4] 'Never do to others what you would not like them to do to you.'[5]

24 The Master said, In speaking of the men of the day I have always refrained from praise and blame alike. But if there is indeed anyone whom I have praised, there is a means by which he may be tested. For the common people here round us are just such stuff as the three dynasties[6] worked upon in the days when they followed the Straight Way.

25 The Master said, I can still remember the days when a scribe left blank spaces,[7] and when someone using a horse (for the first time)[8] hired a man to drive it.[9] But that is all over now!

1 Which contradicts the saying before. As both sayings completely lack context, it would be a waste of time to try to reconcile the contradiction.

2 This is a proverbial saying, capable of many interpretations. To the Taoists it meant 'Seek Tao in yourself (through the practice of quietism) and not in the outside world.'

3 For *chung shên.* cf. IX, 26.

4 . Ch. IV, 15.   5   cf. V, II.   6   Hsia, Yin and Chou.

7 When in doubt; instead of trusting to his imagination.

8 Some such words must have slipped out. Pao Hsien's (first century AD) commentary suggests that they were still there in his text.

9 Another instance of diffidence, parallel to 'leaving blanks'. See additional notes.

26 The Master said, Clever talk can confound the workings of moral force, just as small impatiences can confound great projects.

27 The Master said, When everyone dislikes a man, enquiry is necessary; when everyone likes a man, enquiry is necessary.

28 The Master said, A man can enlarge his Way; but there is no Way that can enlarge a man.[1]

29 The Master said, To have faults and to be making no effort to amend them is to have faults indeed![2]

30 The Master said, I once spent a whole day without food and a whole night without sleep, in order to meditate.[3] It was no use. It is better to learn.[4]

31 The Master said, A gentleman, in his plans, thinks of the Way; he does not think how he is going to make a living. Even farming sometimes entails[5] times of shortage; and even learning may incidentally lead to high pay. But a gentleman's anxieties concern the progress of the Way; he has no anxiety concerning poverty.

32 The Master said, He whose wisdom brings him into power, needs Goodness to secure that power. Else, though he get it, he will certainly lose it. He whose wisdom brings him into power and who has Goodness whereby to secure that power, if he has not dignity wherewith to approach the common people, they will not respect him. He whose wisdom has brought him into

---

1 Without effort on his part. Play on 'Way' and 'road'. 'A man can widen a road . . . ,' etc.

2 Whereas one should never condemn one who is amending his faults. The *Ku-liang Chuan* (Hsi, 22) adds two words, which give a very different turn to the saying.

3 See II, 15.

4 This paragraph reads at first sight as though it were the record of a personal experience. In reality it is meant in a much more general way. *Hsün Tzu* (P'ien, i, fol. 2) quotes the proverb 'I spent a whole day meditating; I should have done better to learn. I stood on tip-toe in order to get a good view; I should have done better to climb a hill.'

5 For the idiom, see II, 18; VII, 15; XIII, 18 and XIX, 6,

power, who has Goodness whereby to secure that power and dignity wherewith to approach the common people, if he handle them contrary to the prescriptions of ritual, is still a bad ruler.[1]

33 The Master said, It is wrong for a gentleman to have knowledge of menial matters[2] and proper that he should be entrusted with great responsibilities. It is wrong for a small man to be entrusted with great responsibilities, but proper that he should have a knowledge of menial matters.

34 The Master said, Goodness is more to the people than water and fire. I have seen men lose their lives when 'treading upon' water and fire; but I have never seen anyone lose his life through 'treading upon' Goodness.[3]

35 The Master said, When it comes to Goodness one need not avoid competing with one's teacher.

36 The Master said, From a gentleman consistency is expected, but not blind fidelity.

37 The Master said, In serving one's prince one should be

> Intent upon the task,
> Not bent upon the pay.

1 This paragraph with its highly literary, somewhat empty elaboration, and its placing of ritual on a pinnacle far above Goodness, is certainly one of the later additions to the book. For the chain-like rhetorical development, cf. XIII, 3.

2 The usual interpretation is 'It is impossible for us to recognise a gentleman when he is merely employed in small matters'. But I do not see how such a sense can be forced out of the text as it stands. For the undesirability of a gentleman's having miscellaneous accomplishments, cf. IX, 6.

3 A symbolic 'treading upon fire' is still used in China as a rite of purification. According to the Lun-hêng (P'ien, 45) a processional wading along the river was part of the rain-making ceremony. Confucius says that Goodness (on the part of the ruler) is a greater and safer purifier than even water or fire.

38   The Master said, There is a difference [1] in instruction but none in kind.

39. The Master said, With those who follow a different Way it is useless to take counsel.

40   The Master said, In official speeches [2] all that matters is to get one's meaning through.

41   The Music-master Mien came to see him. When he reached the steps, the Master said, Here are the steps. [3] When he reached the mat, the Master said, Here is the mat. When everyone was seated the Master informed him saying, So-and-so is here, So-and-so is there. When the Music-master Mien had gone, Tzu-chang asked saying, 'Is that the recognised way to talk to a Music-master?' The Master said, Yes, certainly it is the recognised way to help a Music-master.

1   Between us and the Sages. Any of us could turn into a Yao or Shun, if we trained ourselves as they did. cf. XVII, 2, and *Mencius*, II, A, 2.

2   *Tz'u* means pleas, messages, excuses for being unable to attend to one's duties, etc.

3   Music-masters were blind.

BOOK SIXTEEN

1   (1) The Head of the Chi Family decided to attack Chuan-yü.[1] (2) Jan Ch'iu and Tzu-lu[2] came to see Master K'ung and said to him, The Head of the Chi Family has decided to take steps with regard to Chuan-yü. (3) Master K'ung said, Ch'iu, I fear you must be held responsible for this crime. (4) Chuan-yü was long ago appointed by the Former Kings[3] to preside over the sacrifices to Mount Tung-mêng. Moreover, it lies within the boundaries of our State, and its ruler is a servant of our own Holy Ground and Millet. How can such an attack be justified?

   (5) Jan Ch'iu said, It is our employer who desires it. Neither of us two ministers desires it. (6) Master K'ung said, Ch'iu, among the sayings of Chou Jen[4] there is one which runs: 'He who can bring his powers into play steps into the ranks;[5] he who cannot, stays behind.' Of what use to anyone are such counsellors as you, who see your master tottering, but do not give him a hand, see him falling, but do not prop him up? (7) Moreover, your plea is a false one. For if a tiger or wild buffalo escapes from its cage or a precious ornament of tortoise-shell or jade gets broken in its box, whose fault is it?[6]

1   A small independent State within the borders of Lu.
2   Who were in the service of the Chi Family.
3   The Chou Emperors.
4   An ancient sage. Further sayings by him are quoted in *Tso Chuan*, Yin Kung, 6th year, and Chao Kung, 5th year. I fancy he is the same person as the Ch'ih Jên of the *Shu Ching* (P'an Kêng, Part 1).
5   Military metaphor, here applied to politics.
6   i.e. it is the fault of the person in charge of these things.

(8) Jan Ch'iu said, The present situation is this: Chuan-yü is strongly fortified and is close to Pi.[1] If he does not take it now, in days to come it will certainly give trouble to his sons or grandsons. (9) Master K'ung said, Ch'iu, a true gentleman, having once denied that he is in favour of a course, thinks it wrong to make any attempt to condone that course. (10) Concerning the head of a State or Family I have heard the saying:

> He is not concerned lest his people should be poor,
> But only lest what they have should be ill-apportioned.
> He is not concerned lest they should be few,
> But only lest they should be divided against one another.[2]

And indeed, if all is well-apportioned, there will be no poverty; if they are not divided against one another, there will be no lack of men.[3] (1) If such a state of affairs exists, yet the people of far-off lands still do not submit, then the ruler must attract them by enhancing the prestige (te) of his culture; and when they have been duly attracted, he contents them. And where there is contentment there will be no upheavals.

(12) Today with you two, Yu and Ch'iu, acting as counsellors to your master, the people of far lands do not submit to him, and he is not able to attract them. The State itself is divided and tottering, disrupted and cleft, but he can do nothing to save it and is now planning to wield buckler and axe within the borders of his own land. I am afraid that the troubles of the Chi Family are due not to what is happening in Chuan-yü, but to what is going on behind the screen-wall of his own gate.[4]

2   Master K'ung said, When the Way prevails under Heaven all orders concerning ritual, music and punitive expeditions are issued by the Son of Heaven himself. When the Way does not

1   The chief castle of the Chi Family.
2   The text of this little poem is slightly corrupt.
3   The words *an wu ch'ing* have become displaced. They belong after *an chih*, 21 characters further on.
4   His own lack of *te* and the fact that he has bad advisers.

prevail, such orders are issued by the feudal princes; and when this happens, it is to be observed that ten generations rarely pass before the dynasty falls. If such orders are issued by State Ministers, five generations rarely pass before they lose their power. When the retainers[1] of great Houses seize a country's commission,[2] three generations rarely pass before they lose their power. When the Way prevails under Heaven, policy is not decided by Ministers; when the Way prevails under Heaven, commoners[3] do not discuss public affairs.

3   Master K'ung said, Power over the exchequer was lost by the Ducal House[4] five generations ago, and government has been in the hands of Ministers[5] for four generations. Small wonder that the descendants of the Three Huan[6] are fast losing their power!

4   Master K'ung said, There are three sorts of friend that are profitable, and three sorts that are harmful. Friendship with the upright, with the true-to-death and with those who have heard much is profitable. Friendship with the obsequious, friendship with those who are good at accommodating their principles, friendship with those who are clever at talk is harmful.

5   Master K'ung said, There are three sorts of pleasure that are profitable, and three sorts of pleasure that are harmful. The pleasure got from the due ordering of ritual and music, the

---

1   Such as Yang Huo, who seized power in Lu in 505 BC.
2   The *ming* of a State is the charge whereby the Emperor appoints its feudal lord.
3   People not belonging to the Imperial family.
4   Surrendered by the Duke to the Three Families.
5   The heads of the Chi Family. The first three paragraphs of this book seem to form a connected unity. It was under Chi K'ang-tzu (succeeded in 492 BC) that Tzu-lu and Jan Ch'iu were colleagues. If we take paragraph 3 as having been spoken subsequent to 492 BC, the five powerless Dukes must be Ch'êng, Hsiang, Chao, Ting and Ai; and the four Ministers, Chi Wu-tzu, Chi P'ing-tzu, Chi Huan-tzu and Chi K'ang-tzu. But it would be a mistake to try to fit into too strict a chronology sayings that may be purely legendary.
6   The Three Families, Chi, Mêng and Shu.

pleasure got from discussing the good points in the conduct of others, the pleasure of having many wise friends is profitable. But pleasure got from profligate enjoyments, pleasure got from idle gadding about, pleasure got from comfort and ease is harmful.

6 Master K'ung said, There are three mistakes that are liable to be made when waiting upon a gentleman. To speak before being called upon to do so; this is called forwardness. Not to speak when called upon to do so; this is called secretiveness. To speak without first noting the expression of his face; this is called 'blindness'.[1]

7 Master K'ung said, There are three things against which a gentleman is on his guard. In his youth, before his blood and vital humours[2] have settled down, he is on his guard against lust. Having reached his prime, when the blood and vital humours have finally hardened, he is on his guard against strife. Having reached old age, when the blood and vital humours are already decaying, he is on his guard against avarice.

8 Master K'ung said, There are three things that a gentleman fears: he fears the will of Heaven, he fears great men,[3] he fears the words of the Divine Sages. The small man does not know the will of Heaven and so does not fear it. He treats great men with contempt, and scoffs at the words of the Divine Sages.

9 Master K'ung said, Highest are those who are born wise. Next are those who become wise by learning. After them come those who have to toil painfully in order to acquire learning. Finally, to the lowest class of the common people belong those who toil painfully without ever managing to learn.

1   cf. *Hsün Tzu*, P'ien, 1, end.
2   The physiological theories which underlie this paragraph are, I suspect, considerably posterior to Confucius.
3   *Ta-jen* means (1) giants; (2) ministers, persons in authority; (3) morally great, as in *Mencius*, IV, B, 6; 11 and 12, etc. Probably the meaning here is 'morally great'; that is to say, people like Confucius himself.

10 Master K'ung said, The gentleman has nine cares. In seeing he is careful to see clearly, in hearing he is careful to hear distinctly, in his looks he is careful to bc kindly; in his manner to be respectful, in his words to be loyal, in his work to be diligent. When in doubt he is careful to ask for information; when angry he has a care for the consequences, and when he sees a chance of gain, he thinks carefully whether the pursuit of it would be consonant with the Right.

11, 12 Master K'ung said, 'When they see what is good, they grasp at it as though they feared it would elude them. When they see what is not good, they test it cautiously, as though putting a finger into hot water.' I have heard this saying; I have even seen such men.[1] 'It is by dwelling in seclusion that they seek the fulfilment of their aims; it is by deeds of righteousness that they extend the influence of their Way.' I have heard this saying; but I have never seen such men. 'Duke Ching of Ch'i had a thousand teams of horses; but on the day of his death the people could think of no good deed for which to praise him.[2] Po I and Shu Ch'i[3] starved at[4] the foot of Mount Shou-yang; yet the people sing their praises down to this very day.' Does not this saying illustrate the other?[5]

13 Tzu-ch'in[6] questioned Po Yü[7] saying, As his son[8] you must after

1   These two clauses are accidentally inverted in the original.
2   This is clearly the same formula as VIII, 1 (end), where, however, it is used in praise and not, as here, in condemnation.
3   See V, 22.
4   This form of the preposition, which occurs twice here but nowhere else in the *Analects*, marks the passage as a quotation from some other text. Moreover, the passage is closed by a formula (*ch'i ssu chih wei*) which regularly follows quotations.
5   i.e. are not Po I and Shu Ch'i examples of people who dwelt in seclusion to fulfil their aims, by deeds of righteousness extended the influence of the Way?
6   See I, 10.
7   Confucius's son; see XI, 7.
8   *Tzu* here means 'son' and not 'you, my master'.

all surely have heard something different from what the rest of us hear. Po Yü replied saying, No. Once when he was standing alone and I was hurrying[1] past him across the courtyard, he said, Have you studied the *Songs*? I replied saying, No. (He said) If you do not study the *Songs*, you will find yourself at a loss in conversation. So I retired and studied the *Songs*. Another day he was again standing alone, and as I hurried across the courtyard, he said, Have you studied the rituals? I replied saying, No. (He said) If you do not study the rituals, you will find yourself at a loss how to take your stand.[2] So I retired and studied the rituals. These two things I heard from him.

Tzu-ch'in came away delighted, saying, I asked about one point, but got information about three. I learnt about the *Songs,* about the rituals, and also learnt that a gentleman keeps his son at a distance.[3]

14 The wife of the ruler of a State is referred to by the ruler as 'That person'. She refers to herself as Little Boy. The people of the country call her 'That person of the Prince's'. When speaking of her to people of another State the ruler calls her 'This lonely one's little prince'. But people of another State likewise call her 'That person of the Prince's'.[4]

1 As a sign of respect.
2 On public occasions.
3 The reasons why a gentleman must not teach his own son are discussed in *Mencius*, IV, A, 16. There is a definite ritual severance between father and son. A father may not carry his son in his arms. A son may not, when sacrifice is being made to his deceased father, act as the 'medium' into whom the spirit of the deceased passes. See *Li Chi*, I, fol. 5.
4 This paragraph is a passage on etiquette from some old handbook of ritual, and was probably inserted here merely because it was found along with the manuscript of this *p'ien* (chapter). See additional notes, and cf. *Li Chi*, II, fol. 3.

BOOK SEVENTEEN

1   Yang Huo[1] wanted to see Master K'ung; but Master K'ung would not see him. He sent Master K'ung a sucking pig. Master K'ung, choosing a time when he knew Yang Huo would not be at home, went to tender acknowledgment; but met him in the road. He spoke to Master K'ung, saying, Come here, I have something to say to you. What he said was, Can one who hides his jewel[2] in his bosom and lets his country continue to go astray be called Good? Certainly not. Can one who longs to take part in affairs, yet time after time misses the opportunity to do so — can such a one be called wise? Certainly not.[3] The days and months go by, the years do not wait upon our bidding. Master K'ung said, All right;[4] I am going to serve.

2   The Master said, By nature, near together; by practice far apart.[5]

3   The Master said, It is only the very wisest and the very stupidest who cannot change.

1   See XVI, 2, note. For the anecdote, cf. *Mencius*, III, B, 7.
2   i.e. his talents. cf. XV, 6.
3   Yang Huo answers his own rhetorical questions, a common formula in Chinese.
4   The form of assent Confucius uses implies reluctance. This story, like those in Books XVIII and XIII, certainly originated in non-Confucian circles and comes from the same sort of source as the Confucius Anecdotes in the Taoist works *Chuang Tzu* and *Lieh Tzu*.
5   This proverbial saying has wide possibilities of application. It here presumably means that goodness is a matter of training and application and not an inborn quality.

4   When the Master went to the walled town of Wu,[1] he heard the sound of stringed instruments and singing. Our Master said with a gentle smile, 'To kill a chicken one does not use an ox-cleaver.'[2] Tzu-yu replied saying, I remember once hearing you say, 'A gentleman who has studied the Way will be all the tenderer towards his fellow-men; a commoner who has studied the Way will be all the easier to employ.' The Master said, My disciples, what he says is quite true. What I said just now was only meant as a joke.

5   Kung-shan Fu-jao,[3] when he was holding the castle of Pi in revolt (against the Chi Family), sent for the Master, who would have liked to go; but Tzu-lu did not approve of this and said to the Master, After having refused in so many cases, why go to Kung-shan of all people? The Master said, It cannot be for nothing[4] that he has sent for me. If anyone were to use me, I believe I could make a 'Chou in the east'.[5]

6   Tzu-chang asked Master K'ung about Goodness. Master K'ung said, He who could put the Five into practice everywhere under Heaven would be Good. Tzu-chang begged to hear what these were. The Master said, Courtesy, breadth, good faith, diligence and clemency. 'He who is courteous is not scorned, he who is broad wins the multitude, he who is of good faith is trusted by

1   Where Tzu-yu was in command. See VI, 12.
2   A saying of proverbial type meaning, in effect, that in teaching music to the inhabitants of this small town Tzu-yu is 'casting pearls before swine'. The proverb may well have had a second, balancing clause, here alluded to, but not expressed; such as, 'To teach commoners one does not use a zithern.'
3   Warden of Pi, the chief stronghold of the Chi Family. He revolted in 502 BC, but in 498 BC he fled to Ch'i and later to Wu where he is said to have plotted, in a spirit of petty revenge, against his native State of Lu.
4   Confucius believes that Kung-shan intends to restore the Duke to his rightful powers.
5   Create a second Golden Age, comparable to the early days of the Chou dynasty.

the people, he who is diligent succeeds in all he undertakes, he who is clement can get service from the people.'[1]

7 Pi Hsi[2] summoned the Master, and he would have liked to go. But Tzu-lu said, I remember your once saying, 'Into the house of one who is in his own person doing what is evil, the gentleman will not enter.' Pi Hsi is holding Chung-mou[3] in revolt. How can you think of going to him? The Master said, It is true that there is such a saying. But is it not also said that there are things 'So hard that no grinding will ever wear them down', that there are things 'So white that no steeping will ever make them black'? Am I indeed to be forever like the bitter gourd that is only fit to hang up,[4] but not to eat?[5]

8 The Master said, Yu, have you ever been told of the Six Sayings about the Six Degenerations? Tzu-lu replied, No, never. (The Master said) Come, then; I will tell you. Love of Goodness without love of learning[6] degenerates into silliness. Love of wisdom without love of learning degenerates into utter lack of principle. Love of keeping promises without love of learning degenerates into villainy.[7] Love of uprightness without love of learning[8] degenerates into harshness. Love of courage without love of learning degenerates into turbulence.[9] Love of courage without love of learning degenerates into mere recklessness.

---

1 This is almost certainly a quotation from some text of the *Shu Ching*. cf. XX, 1, where most of it reappears.
2 A Chin officer.
3 A town in Wei, captured by the Chin (in 490?).
4 Till it is dry and can be used as a vessel.
5 Play on two senses of *shih* (1) to eat; (2) to get a salary, an official post.
6 i.e. learning the Way of the ancients.
7 i.e. keeping regrettable pacts and promises to the detriment of *i* (what is right under the circumstances).
8 Like that of Upright Kung, XIII, 18.
9 The tendency to fling oneself into any revolutions or upheavals that are going on in the world around one.

9   The Master said, Little ones, Why is it that none of you study the *Songs*? For the *Songs* will help you to incite people's emotions, to observe their feelings, to keep company, to express your grievances. They may be used at home in the service of one's father; abroad, in the service of one's prince.[1] Moreover, they will widen your acquaintance with the names[2] of birds, beasts, plants and trees.

10   The Master addressed Po Yü[3] saying, Have you done the *Chou Nan* and the *Shao Nan*[4] yet? He who has not even done the *Chou Nan* and the *Shao Nan* is as though he stood with his face pressed against a wall!

11   The Master said, Ritual, ritual! Does it mean no more than presents of jade and silk?[5] Music, music! Does it mean no more than bells and drums?

12   The Master said, To assume an outward air of fierceness when inwardly trembling is (to take a comparison from low walks of life) as dishonest as to sneak into places where one has no right to be, by boring a hole or climbing through a gap.

13   The Master said, The 'honest villager' spoils[6] true virtue (*te*).

14   The Master said, To tell in the lane what you have heard on the highroad is to throw merit (*te*) away.

15   The Master said, How could one ever possibly serve one's prince alongside of such low-down creatures? Before they have got office, they think about nothing but how to get it; and when they have got it, all they care about is to avoid losing it. And so soon as they see themselves in the slightest danger of losing it, there is no length to which they will not go.

---

1   For the uses of the *Songs* here inculcated, see *The Book of Songs*, p 335.
2   i.e. the 'correct names', the names in the ancient Court dialect used in ritual, as opposed to the local names.
3   Son of Confucius. See XVI, 13.
4   The first two books of the *Songs*.
5   cf. *Hsün Tzu*, P'ien, 27, fol. 1.
6   As we should say 'Spoils the market for . . . ' For a long discussion of this saying, see *Mencius*, VII, B, 37.

16 In old days the common people had three faults, part[1] of which
    they have now lost. In old days the impetuous were merely
    impatient of small restraints; now they are utterly insubordinate.
    In old days the proud were stiff and formal; now they are touchy
    and quarrelsome. In old days simpletons were at any rate
    straightforward; but now 'simple-mindedness' exists only as a
    device of the impostor.

17 The Master said, Clever talk and a pretentious manner are
    seldom found in the Good.[2]

18 The Master said, I hate to see roan killing red, I hate to see the
    tunes of Chëng[3] corrupting Court music, I hate to see sharp
    mouths overturning kingdoms and clans.

19 The Master said, I would much rather not have to talk. Tzu-
    kung said, If our Master did not talk, what should we little ones
    have to hand down about him? The Master said, Heaven does
    not speak; yet the four seasons run their course thereby,[4] the
    hundred creatures, each after its kind, are born thereby. Heaven
    does no speaking!

20 Ju Pei[5] wanted to see Master K'ung. Master K'ung excused
    himself on the ground of ill-health. But when the man who had
    brought the message was going out through the door he took up
    his zithern and sang, taking good care that the messenger should
    hear.

1   What follows is a paradox, for we expect to hear that the people have
    improved; whereas it turns out that the 'lost parts' were redeeming
    features.
2   Identical with I, 3.
3   See XV, 10. cf. also *Mencius*, VII, B, 37.
4   By command of Heaven.
5   Of whom practically nothing is known. He had evidently disgraced
    himself.

21 Tsai Yü[1] asked about the three years' mourning,[2] and said he thought a year would be quite long enough: 'If gentlemen suspend their practice of the rites[3] for three years, the rites will certainly decay; if for three years they make no music, music will certainly be destroyed.'[4] (In a year) the old crops have already vanished, the new crops have come up, the whirling drills have made new fire.[5] Surely a year would be enough?

The Master said, Would you then (after a year) feel at ease in eating good rice and wearing silk brocades? Tsai Yü said, Quite at ease. (The Master said) If you would really feel at ease, then do so. But when a true gentleman is in mourning, if he eats dainties, he does not relish them, if he hears music, it does not please him, if he sits in his ordinary seat, he is not comfortable. That is why he abstains from these things. But if you would really feel at ease, there is no need for you to abstain.

When Tsai Yü had gone out, the Master said, How inhuman[6] Yü is! Only when a child is three years old does it leave its parents' arms. The three years' mourning is the universal mourning everywhere under Heaven.[7] And Yü – was he not the darling of his father and mother for three years?

1 See V, 9.

2 For parents. Three years is often interpreted as meaning 'into the third year', i.e. 25 months.

3 The mourning for parents entailed complete suspension of all ordinary activities.

4 A traditional saying. cf. *Shih Chi*, Ch. 28, beginning.

5 The ritualists describe four 'fire-changing' rites, one for each season, the new fire being in each case kindled on the wood of a tree appropriate to the season. But perhaps the only actual 'fire-changing', when all fires were put out and after three days rekindled from a new ritually-obtained flame, was in the spring. See *Hou Han Shu*, LXI, fol. 6, recto and *Chou Li*, Ch. 57 (commentary).

6 *Jen* is here used in its later sense, 'possessing human feelings', 'kind'. This chapter shows many signs of late date.

7 The whole object of this paragraph is to claim Confucius as a supporter of the three years' mourning. This custom was certainly far from being 'universal', and was probably not ancient. cf. *Mencius* III, A, 3, where the people of Têng protest that even in Lu 'the former princes none of them practised it'.

22 The Master said, Those who do nothing all day but cram themselves with food and never use their minds are difficult.[1] Are there not games such as draughts?[2] To play them would surely be better than doing nothing at all.

23 Tzu-lu said, Is courage to be prized by a gentleman? The Master said, A gentleman gives the first place to Right. If a gentleman has courage but neglects Right, he becomes turbulent. If a small man has courage but neglects Right, he becomes a thief.

24 Tzu-kung said, Surely even the gentleman must have his hatreds. The Master said, He has his hatreds. He hates those who point out what is hateful in others.[3] He hates those who dwelling in low estate[4] revile all who are above them. He hates those who love deeds of daring but neglect ritual. He hates those who are active and venturesome, but are violent in temper. I suppose you also have your hatreds? Tzu-kung said,[5] I hate those who mistake cunning for wisdom. I hate those who mistake insubordination for courage. I hate those who mistake tale-bearing for honesty.

25 The Master said, Women and people of low birth are very hard to deal with. If you are friendly with them, they get out of hand, and if you keep your distance, they resent it.[6]

26 The Master said, One who has reached the age of forty and is still disliked will be so till the end.

---

1 cf. XV, 16.
2 For draughts, see *Tso Chuan*, Duke Hsiang, 25th year, end. It no doubt resembled the current game of *wei-ch'i*. I think *po* (cognate with *po* 'to strike', cf. Japanese *utsu*, 'to strike', i.e. make a move in board-games) is to be taken with *i* and is not the name of a separate game.
3 cf. *Kuan Tzu*, P'ien, 66, end.
4 *liu* has been wrongly inserted here on the analogy of XIX, 20.
5 This 'said' has accidentally been transferred to the clause above.
6 Like Liu Pao-nan, I take *nü-tzu* in its ordinary sense of 'women' as opposed to 'men', and *hsiao jen* in its ordinary sense of 'cads' as opposed to 'gentlemen'. The standard interpreters soften the saying by making it apply to 'maids and valets'.

BOOK EIGHTEEN

1   'The lord of Wei fled from him,[1] the lord of Chi suffered slavery at his hands, Pi Kan rebuked him and was slain.' Master K'ung said, In them the Yin had three Good men.

2   When Liu-hsia Hui[2] was Leader of the Knights,[3] he was three times dismissed. People said to him, Surely you would do well to seek service elsewhere? He said, If I continue to serve men in honest ways, where can I go and not be three times dismissed? If, on the other hand, I am willing to serve men by crooked ways, what need is there for me to leave the land of my father and mother?

3   Duke Ching of Ch'i received Master K'ung; he said, To treat him on an equality with the head of the Chi Family is impossible. I will receive him as though he ranked between the head of the Chi and the head of the Mêng. (At the interview) he said, I am old and have no use for you. Whereupon Master K'ung left (the land of Ch'i).[4]

1   i.e. from the tyrant Chou, last sovereign of the Yin dynasty. The lord of Wei was his step-brother. The lord of Chi and Pi Kan were his uncles.

2   See XV, 13.

3   A comparatively humble post. Its occupant was chiefly concerned with criminal cases.

4   Book XVIII is wholly legendary in content. The Confucius who ranked above the head of the Mêng family is already well on the way towards apotheosis.

4 The people of Ch'i sent to Lu a present of female musicians,[1] and Chi Huan-tzu[2] accepted them. For three days no Court was held, whereupon Master K'ung left Lu.

5 Chieh Yü,[3] the madman of Ch'u, came past Master K'ung, singing as he went:

> Oh phoenix, phoenix
> How dwindled is your power!
> As to the past, reproof is idle,
> But the future may yet be remedied.
> Desist, desist!
> Great in these days is the peril of those who fill office.

Master K'ung got down,[4] desiring to speak with him; but the madman hastened his step and got away, so that Master K'ung did not succeed in speaking to him.

6 Ch'ang-chü and Chieh-ni[5] were working as plough-mates together. Master K'ung, happening to pass that way, told Tzu-lu to go and ask them where the river could be forded. Ch'ang-chü said, Who is it for whom you are driving? Tzu-lu said, For K'ung Ch'iu. He said, What, K'ung Ch'iu of Lu? Tzu-lu said, Yes, he. Ch'ang-chü said, In that case he already knows where the ford is.[6] Tzu-lu then asked Chieh-ni. Chieh-ni said, Who are you? He said, I am Tzu-lu. Chien-ni said, You are a follower of K'ung Ch'iu of Lu, are you not? He said, That is so. Chieh-ni said, Under Heaven there is none that is not swept along by the

---

1 In order to weaken the power of the government. A common folk-lore theme.

2 The father of Chi K'ang-tzu; died 492 BC. This is the only passage in the *Analects* where he is directly mentioned.

3 See *Chuang Tzu*, IV, 8, where this typically Taoist, anti-Confucian story is told in a slightly longer form. For the 'madman', see also *Chuang Tzu*, I, 4 and VII, 2, *Hsin Hsü*, III. *Han Fei Tzu*, P'ien, 20. *Chan Kuo T'sê*, Ch'in stories, Pt. II.

4 From his carriage.

5 The names recall in their formation those of the fictitious personages in *Chuang Tzu* and *Lieh Tzu*.

6 Or should do; for he claims to be a Sage.

same flood. Such is the world and who can change it? As for you, instead of following one who flees from this man and that, you would do better to follow one who shuns this whole generation of men. And with that he went on covering the seed.

Tzu-lu went and told his master, who said ruefully, One cannot herd with birds and beasts. If I am not to be a man among other men, then what am I to be?[1] If the Way prevailed under Heaven, I should not be trying to alter things.

7 Once when Tzu-lu was following (the Master) he fell behind and met an old man carrying a basket[2] slung over his staff. Tzu-lu asked him, saying, Sir, have you seen my master? The old man said, You who

> With your four limbs do not toil,
> Who do not sift the five grains,[3]

who is your master? And with that he planted his staff in the ground and began weeding, while Tzu-lu stood by with his hands pressed together.[4]

He kept Tzu-lu for the night, killed a fowl, prepared a dish of millet for his supper and introduced him to his two sons. Tzu-lu said, It is not right to refuse to serve one's country. The laws of age and youth may not be set aside. And how can it be right for a man to set aside the duty that binds minister to prince, or in his desire to maintain his own integrity, to subvert the Great Relationship?[5] A gentleman's service to his country consists in doing such right as he can. That the Way does not prevail, he knows well enough beforehand.

Next day[6] Tzu-lu went on his way and reported what had

1 I think the second *yü*, like the first, is interrogative.   2 cf. XIV, 20.
3 Who would not know how to choose the right seed for sowing. The five kinds of grain are rice, two kinds of millet, wheat and pulse.
4 The palms pressed together in an attitude of respect.
5 This is the only book in the *Analects* in which the term *lun* (relationship) which figures so prominently in later Confucianism, makes its appearance.
6 In the original this clause down to 'gone away' follows the words 'his two sons'. This makes the whole story run very awkwardly; see T.T. 2036. The clauses have certainly become accidentally inverted.

happened. The Master said, He is a recluse, and told Tzu-lu to go back and visit him again. But on arriving at the place he found that the old man had gone away.[1]

8   Subjects whose services were lost to the State: Po I, Shu Ch'i,[2] Yü Chung,[3] I I, Chu Chang,[4] Liu-hsia Hui, Shao Lien.[5] The Master said, Those of them who 'would neither abate their high resolve nor bring humiliation upon themselves' were, I suppose, Po I and Shu Ch'i. It means that[6] Liu-hsia Hui and Shao Lien did abate their high resolve and bring humiliation upon themselves. 'Their words were consonant with the Relationships, their deeds were consonant with prudence; this and no more,' means that Yü Chung and I I, on the contrary, lived in seclusion and refrained from comment. They secured personal integrity; and when set aside maintained due balance.[7] As for me, I am different from any of these. I have no 'thou shalt' or 'thou shalt not'.

9   The Chief Musician Chih[8] betook himself to Ch'i; Kan, the leader of the band at the second meal,[9] betook himself to Ch'u, Liao (leader of the band at the third meal) went to Ts'ai, and

---

1   Fearing that Confucius might recommend him for public service? Compare the very similar story, *Chuang Tzu*, XXV, 5.

2   For Po I and Shu Ch'i, see V, 22.

3   Brother of T'ai Po, VIII, 1.

4   I I and Chu Chang are unknown. I suspect that Chu Chang at any rate is not a proper name at all, but a corruption of part of the sentence. This was clearly suspected by Lu Tê-ming (*c.* AD 600).

5   For Liu-hsia Hui, see XV, 13. Shao-lien is said to have been an 'eastern barbarian'.

6   Confucius seems here to be commenting on some text which is unknown to us.

7   This whole paragraph is certainly corrupt. Liu-hsia Hui hung on to office despite every rebuff, and cannot be counted as a 'lost subject'. After the name of I I some phrase must have followed meaning, 'those who concealed their discontent', or the like.

8   cf. VIII, 15. It is natural to suppose that this migration took place when Duke Chao of Lu fled to Ch'i in 517 BC.

9   Or 'at the second course'.

Ch'üeh (leader of the band at the fourth meal) went to Ch'in. The big drummer Fang Shu went within[1] the River, the kettle-drummer Wu went within the River Han, the Minor Musician Yang and Hsiang, the player of the stone-chimes, went within the sea.[2]

10 The Duke of Chou addressed the Duke of Lu,[3] saying: A gentleman never discards[4] his kinsmen; nor does he ever give occasion to his chief retainers to chafe at not being used. None who have been long in his service does he ever dismiss without grave cause. He does not expect one man to be capable of everything.[5]

11 Chou had its Eight Knights:

Elder-brother Ta	(d'ât)
Elder-brother Kua	(g'uât)
Middle-brother T'u	(t'ut)
Middle-brother Hu	(hut)
Younger-brother Yeh	(zia)
Younger-brother Hsia	(g'a)
Youngest-brother Sui	(d'uâ)
Youngest-brother Kua	(Kuâ)[6]

1   i.e. to the north of.

2   to an island. This paragraph and the two which follow it are stray fragments arbitrarily inserted at the end of the Book. cf. the terminations of Books X and XVI.   3   His son.

4   The original sense of the maxim may have been 'never reserves all his largesses for his own kinsmen'.   5   cf. XIII, 25.

6   A sign that a country had reached the maximum of plenty and fertility was that one woman should bear four pairs of twins. cf. the similar set of twins mentioned in Tsang Wên Chung's great discourse, *Tso Chuan*, Duke Wên, 18th year. The present set is unknown elsewhere, and commentators cannot decide in what reign the happy phenomenon took place. I give the names in their approximate ancient pronunciation, to show that they form a sort of jingle. 'The names go in pairs, as becomes those of twins,' says Huang K'an. For the pronunciation of the last name I follow Lu Tê-ming.

BOOK NINETEEN

1 Tzu-chang said, A knight who confronted with danger is ready to lay down his life, who confronted with the chance of gain thinks first of right, who judges sacrifice by the degree of reverence shown and mourning by the degree of grief [1] – such a one is all that can be desired.

2 Tzu-chang said, He who sides with moral force (*te*) but only to a limited extent,[2] who believes in the Way, but without conviction – how can one count him as with us, how can one count him as not with us?

3 The disciples of Tzu-hsia asked Tzu-chang about intercourse with others. Tzu-chang said, What does Tzu-hsia tell you? He replied saying, Tzu-hsia says:

> Go with those with whom it is proper to go;
> Keep at a distance those whom it is proper to keep at a
>   distance.

Tzu-chang said, That is different from what I have been told:

> A gentleman reverences those that excel, but 'finds
>   room'[3] for all;
> He commends the good and pities the incapable.

---

1 And not by the elaborateness of the ceremonies. For the first part of the saying, cf. XIV, 13.
2 Saying for example that *te* has its uses, but that the ultimate appeal must always be to physical compulsion.
3 i.e. tolerates.

Do I myself greatly excel others? In that case I shall certainly find room for everyone. Am I myself inferior to others? In that case, it would be others who would keep me at a distance. So that the question of keeping others at a distance does not arise.[1]

4   Tzu-hsia said, Even the minor walks[2] (of knowledge) have an importance of their own. But if pursued too far they tend to prove a hindrance; for which reason a gentleman does not cultivate them.

5   Tzu-hsia said, He who from day to day is conscious of what he still lacks, and from month to month never forgets what he has already learnt, may indeed be called a true lover of learning.

6   Tzu-hsia said,

> One who studies widely and with set purpose,
> Who questions earnestly, then thinks for himself about
>   what he has heard

– such a one will incidentally [3] achieve Goodness.

7   Tzu-hsia said, Just as the hundred[4] apprentices must live in workshops to perfect themselves in their craft, so the gentleman studies, that he may improve himself in the Way.

8   Tzu-hsia said, When the small man goes wrong, it is always on the side of over-elaboration.[5]

---

1   Literally, what becomes of that (*ch'i* in such usages corresponds to the Latin *iste*) 'keeping others at a distance' of yours?

2   Such as agriculture, medicine, etc. The idea that specialised knowledge is incompatible with true gentility prevailed in England till well towards the close of the nineteenth century.

3   cf. II, 18; VII, 15; XIII, 18 and XV, 21.

4   i.e. all the different sorts of . . .

5   Lu Tê-ming does not gloss this character, and therefore presumably read *wên* in its ordinary pronunciation. I see no reason to read it in the 'departing tone', with the meaning 'gloss over', 'make excuses'. The sole authority for the usual interpretation is the pseudo K'ung An-kuo.

9   Tzu-hsia said, A gentleman has three varying aspects: seen from afar, he looks severe, when approached he is found to be mild, when heard speaking he turns out to be incisive.

10   Tzu-hsia said, A gentleman obtains the confidence of those under him, before putting burdens upon them. If he does so before he has obtained their confidence, they feel that they are being exploited. It is also true that he obtains the confidence (of those above him) before criticising them. If he does so before he has obtained their confidence, they feel that they are being slandered.

11   Tzu-hsia said, So long as in undertakings of great moral import a man does not 'cross the barrier', in undertakings of little moral import he may 'come out and go in'. [1]

12   Tzu-yu said, Tzu-hsia's disciples and scholars, so long as it is only a matter of sprinkling and sweeping floors, answering summonses and replying to questions, coming forward and retiring, are all right. But these are minor matters. Set them to anything important, and they would be quite at a loss.

    Tzu-hsia, hearing of this, said, Alas, Yen Yu is wholly mistaken. Of the Way of the True Gentleman it is said:

        If it be transmitted to him before he is ripe
        By the time he is ripe, he will weary of it.

    Disciples may indeed be compared to plants and trees. They have to be separately treated according to their kinds.

    In the Way of the Gentleman there can be no bluff. It is only the Divine Sage who embraces in himself both the first step and the last.

1   In matters such as loyalty, keeping promises, obedience to parents, the laws which govern his conduct are absolute. In lesser matters he is allowed a certain latitude. Several early writers attribute the saying to Confucius himself.

13 Tzu-hsia said, The energy that a man has left[1] over after doing his duty to the State, he should devote to study; the energy that he has left after studying, he should devote to service of the State.

14 Tzu-yu said, The ceremonies of mourning should be carried to the extreme that grief dictates, and no further.

15 Tzu-yu said, My friend Chang does 'the things that it is hard to be able to do';[2] but he is not yet Good.

16 Master Tsêng said, Chang is so self-important. It is hard to become Good when working side by side with such a man.

17 Master Tsêng said, I once heard the Master say, Though a man may never before have shown all that is in him, he is certain to do so when mourning for a father or mother.

18 Master Tsêng said, I once heard the Master say, Filial piety such as that of Mêng Chuang Tzu[3] might in other respects be possible to imitate; but the way in which he changed neither his father's[4] servants nor his father's domestic policy, that would indeed be hard to emulate.

19 When the Chief of the Mêng Family[5] appointed Yang Fu as Leader of the Knights,[6] Yang Fu[7] came for advice to Master Tsêng. Master Tsêng said, It is long since those above lost the Way of the Ruler and the common people lost their cohesion. If you find evidence of this, then be sad and show pity rather than be pleased at discovering such evidence.

1 cf. I, 6.
2 cf. XIV, 2.
3 Died in 550 BC.
4 Mêng Hsien Tzu, died in 554 BC.
5 Mêng Wu Po, who succeeded to the headship of the clan in 481 BC. Usually explained as meaning Mêng I Tzu, predecessor of Mêng Wu Po. But in his time (if we are to follow the traditional chronology) Master Tsêng would have been too young to be consulted. It must be remembered, however, that the Confucian legend was not built up by people who had chronological tables open in front of them.
6 A post involving the judging of criminal cases.
7 Unknown.

20 Tzu-kung said, The tyrant Chou[1] cannot really have been as
wicked as all this! That is why a gentleman hates to 'dwell on low
ground'. He knows that all filth under Heaven tends to
accumulate there.

21 Tzu-kung said, The faults of a gentleman are like eclipses of the
sun or moon. If he does wrong, everyone sees it. When he
corrects his fault, every gaze is turned up towards him.

22 Kung-sun Ch'ao of Wei[2] asked Tzu-kung, From whom did
Chung-ni[3] derive his learning? Tzu-kung said, The Way of the
kings Wên and Wu has never yet utterly fallen to the ground.
Among men,[4] those of great understanding have recorded the
major principles of this Way and those of less understanding have
recorded the minor principles. So that there is no one who has
not access to the Way of Wên and Wu. From whom indeed did
our Master *not* learn? But at the same time, what need had he of
any fixed and regular teacher?

23 Shu-sun Wu-shu[5] talking to some high officers at Court said,
Tzu-kung is a better man than Chung-ni. Tzu-fu Ching-po[6]
repeated this to Tzu-kung. Tzu-kung said, Let us take as our
comparison the wall round a building. My wall only reaches to
the level of a man's shoulder, and it is easy enough to peep over it
and see the good points of the house on the other side. But our
Master's wall rises many times a man's height, and no one who is
not let in by the gate can know the beauty and wealth of the
palace that, with its ancestral temple, its hundred ministrants, lies
hidden within. But it must be admitted that those who are let in
by the gate are few; so that it is small wonder His Excellency
should have spoken as he did.

1 See XVIII, 1.
2 So called to distinguish him from a number of Kung-sun Ch'aos in
other countries.
3 i.e. Confucius.
4 The usual interpretation: 'It is still here among men', implies a very
abrupt construction.
5 Flourished c.500 BC.
6 cf. XIV, 38.

24 Shu-sun Wu-shu having spoken disparagingly of Chung-ni, Tzu-kung said, It is no use; Chung-ni cannot be disparaged. There may be other good men; but they are merely like hillocks or mounds that can easily be climbed. Chung-ni is the sun and moon that cannot be climbed over. If a man should try to cut himself off from them, what harm would it do to the sun and moon? It would only show that he did not know his own measure.

25 Tzu-ch'in[1] said to Tzu-kung, This is an affectation of modesty. Chung-ni is in no way your superior. Tzu-kung said, You should be more careful about what you say. A gentleman, though for a single word he may be set down as wise, for a single word is set down as a fool. It would be as hard to equal our Master as to climb up on a ladder to the sky. Had our Master ever been put in control of a State or of a great Family, it would have been as is described in the words: 'He raised them, and they stood, he led them and they went. He steadied them as with a rope, and they came. He stirred them, and they moved harmoniously. His life was glorious, his death bewailed.'[2] How can such a one ever be equalled?

1   See I, 10 and XVI, 13.
2   Probably a quotation from a *lei* (funeral eulogy).

BOOK TWENTY

1   Yao said, Oh you, Shun!

> Upon you in your own person now rests the heavenly
>   succession;[1]
> Faithfully grasp it by the centre.
> The Four Seas may run dry;[2]
> But this heavenly gift lasts forever.

Shun too, when giving his charge to Yü . . . (hiatus).

   (T'ang)[3] said, I, your little son Li, venture to sacrifice a black
ox and tell you, oh most august sovereign God, that those who
are guilty[4] I dare not spare; but God's servants I will not slay. The
decision is in your heart, O God.

   If I in my own person do any wrong, let it never be visited
upon the many lands. But if anywhere in the many lands wrong
be done, let it be visited upon my person.[5]

---

1   See additional notes.
2   i.e. 'sooner shall the sea run dry, than this gift . . . ' For *yung-chung*, cf.
   Shu Ching, Metal Casket, 10.
3   Founder of the Yin dynasty, when informing the Supreme Ancestor of
   his (T'ang's) accession. Li was his personal name.
4   The Hsia, whom T'ang had defeated.
5   This 'scape-goat' formula is constantly referred to in early Chinese
   literature. Mo Tzu (Universal Love, Pt. III), after quoting this same
   passage, says that T'ang 'did not scruple to make of himself a sacrificial
   victim'. The passage has been reinterpreted in a very drastic fashion.

> When Chou gave its great largesses,
> It was the good who were enriched:
> 'Although I have my Chou kinsmen,
> They are less to me than the Good Men.[1]
> If among the many families
> There be one that does wrong,
> Let the wrong be visited on me alone.'

(King Wu)[2] paid strict attention to weights and measures, reviewed the statutes and laws, restored disused offices, and gave a polity to all the four quarters of the world. He raised up States that had been destroyed, re-established lines of succession that had been broken, summoned lost subjects back to prominence, and all the common people under Heaven gave their hearts to him. What he cared for most was that the people should have food, and that the rites of mourning and sacrifice should be fulfilled.

He who is broad[3] wins the multitude, he who keeps his word is trusted by the people, he who is diligent succeeds in all he undertakes, he who is just is the joy (of the people).

2   Tzu-chang asked Master K'ung, saying, What must a man do, that he may thereby be fitted to govern the land? The Master said, He must pay attention to the Five Lovely Things[4] and put away from him the Four Ugly Things. Tzu-chang said, What are they, that you call the Five Lovely Things? The Master said, A gentleman 'can be bounteous without extravagance, can get work out of people without arousing resentment, has longings but is never covetous, is proud but never insolent, inspires awe but is never ferocious'.

Tzu-chang said, What is meant by being bounteous without extravagance? The Master said, If he gives to the people only

---

1   i.e. those who distinguished themselves in the campaign against Yin. The speaker is presumably King Wu.
2   Or the Duke of Chou?
3   'He who is broad' down to 'undertakes' occurs also in XVII, 6.
4   For these enumerations, cf. XVI, 4-8.

such advantages as are really advantageous[1] to them, is he not being bounteous without extravagance? If he imposes upon them only such tasks as they are capable of performing, is he not getting work out of them without arousing resentment? If what he longs for and what he gets is Goodness, who can say that he is covetous? A gentleman, irrespective of whether he is dealing with many persons or with few, with the small or with the great, never presumes to slight them. Is not this indeed being 'proud without insolence'? A gentleman sees to it that his clothes and hat are put on straight, and imparts such dignity to his gaze that he imposes on others. No sooner do they see him from afar than they are in awe. Is not this indeed inspiring awe without ferocity?

Tzu-chang said, What are they, that you call the Four Ugly Things? The Master said, Putting men to death, without having taught them (the Right); that is called savagery. Expecting the completion of tasks, without giving due warning; that is called oppression. To be dilatory about giving orders, but to expect absolute punctuality, that is called being a tormentor. And similarly, though meaning to let a man have something, to be grudging about bringing it out from within, that is called behaving like a petty functionary.

3   The Master said, He who does not understand the will of Heaven cannot be regarded as a gentleman. He who does not know the rites cannot take his stand.[2] He who does not understand words,[3] cannot understand people.

1   For example, if he promotes agriculture instead of distributing doles and largesses.
2   cf. XVI, 13.
3   i.e. cannot get beneath the surface-meaning and understand the state of mind that the words really imply. cf. *Mencius*, II, A, 2. Para. 3 was lacking in the Lu version.

ADDITIONAL NOTES

II, 18   *tsai ch'i chung* is an idiom (cf. VII, 15; XIII, 18; XV, 31 and XIX, 6) which can never be translated literally. It is used of results that occur incidentally without being the main object of a certain course of action.

III, 1   Eight teams of dancers.
          The exact number of performers is in every ritual a matter of extreme importance. The Chi family's crime consisted in usurping rites which were proper only to the Ducal House; or, possibly, proper only to the Emperor. They were 'making the twigs heavy and the trunk light' – the surest way to ruin.

III, 8   An alternative interpretation of Confucius's reply is: 'In painting, the plain colour (i.e. the white) is put on last', because otherwise it would get soiled. This explanation lands us in all kinds of difficulties, and is based, I think, on a misunderstanding of a passage in the *Chou Li*, LXXIX (p. 17; Biot's translation, II, 516, which in reality means: 'When birds, beasts and snakes are combined with the symbols of the four seasons and with the five colours in their proper arrangements, and are thus duly displayed, this is called "skilled work". In the business of painting (i.e. of decorating the personal possessions of officials with designs appropriate to their rank) plain work comes after (i.e. is not considered so highly).'
          'Plain work' is painted in the appropriate colours, but lacks the birds, beasts and snakes that decorate the appurtenances of the mighty. Confucius uses the same maxim as the Chou Li, but reinterprets it as meaning not

'In painting plain work is not so highly esteemed', but 'The painting comes after the plain groundwork'.

The *Chou Li* commentary tries to force upon 'plain work' the impossible sense of 'application of white pigment', thus making the last sentence totally disconnected from the context.

III, 15   The poem *T'ien Wên* is supposed to embody the questions asked by the poet Ch'ü Yüan when he visited the shrines of former kings and ministers, and to concern legends depicted on the walls of these shrines.

III, 16   According to the *Chou Li* (XXI, 52) the local archery meeting was made the occasion for a general review of conduct, 'points' in the competition being given for (1) not quarrelling; (2) correct deportment; (3) *chu-p'i*, explained as meaning 'skill in archery'; (4) singing; (5) dancing.

It is clear, then, that the *Chou Li* does not give to *chu* the meaning 'give chief place to'; it is, however, equally clear that in the *Lun Yü* passage *chu* can only bear this meaning. Moreover, the mention in *Lun Yü* of 'strength' suggests that 'piercing the hide' and not merely hitting the mark is what is meant.

III, 21   *Shê* (holy ground) was an earth-mound at the borders of a town or village, interpreted as symbolising the whole soil of the territory in which it stood. It was often associated with a sacred tree or grove, and with a block or pillar of wood[1] which served as a 'stance' (resting-place) for spirits. This wooden object was called *chu*.

In parallel passages the question at issue is what sort of wood was used in making the *chu*. This passage is generally taken as referring to the trees of the Holy Ground and not to the material of the *chu*.

The *feng*, a terminal earth-mound where a road reached

1   In other parts of the world objects analogous to the *chu* vary within comparatively small areas between being made of stone and being made of wood. The typical Chinese *chu* has always been a wooden object; but *chu* of other materials including stone probably also existed.

the borders of a State, is analogous to the *shê*, and the same official was responsible for the maintenance of both.

IV, 11   The Chu Hsi interpretation is 'The gentleman thinks of *te*, the small man of material comfort; the gentleman, of punishments (i.e. justice); the small man of favours.' In his conversations (section on *Lun Yü* in *Chu Tzu Ch'üan Shu*) he records that Yin Shun (AD 1071–1142) construed the sentence as I have done; and Huang K'an (sixth century) notes this rendering as an alternative one. The absence of any 'then', 'in that case' in the second and fourth clauses makes the sentence obscure, and I fancy that *tsê* (then) has been suppressed in order to admit of an interpretation such as Chu Hsi's, by people who unlike Confucius, believed in government by penalties. Chu Hsi's interpretation of *huai-t'u* is hopelessly forced.

IV, 26   The character that I have translated 'repeated scolding' means literally 'to enumerate'. Hence to 'enumerate people's faults', to 'tick off'. cf. *Shih Chi*, ch. 86, fol. 4.

    It is taken in this sense here by Yü Yüeh[1] (died AD 1906). The *Chi Chieh* gives it the meaning 'quick', 'hasty'. cf. *Lieh Tzu*, II, 8: 'Anyone who is good at swimming can quickly learn . . . ', and *Chuang Tzu*, XIX, 4. But Chêng Hsüan, the great Han dynasty commentator, explains it as meaning 'enumerating one's own services'. Finally, the current explanation gives it the meaning 'numerously', 'repeatedly'. Comparison with XII, 23 seems to show that this last explanation is right.

V, 2   For this saying, set in the context of a longer anecdote, see *K'ung Tzu Chia Yü*, XIX (Tzu-lu Ch'u Chien) and *Shuo Yüan*, VII. A work called *Fu Tzu* (i.e. sayings of Master Fu) was current until the first century AD, and the stories about Fu's ideal governorship which are found in works of the third century BC and onwards may be extracts from Fu Tzu. See G. Haloun, *Asia Major*, VIII, fasc. 3, pp. 437 seq. But there is no reason to suppose that any of these stories

1   H. P. 1391, 10.

supplies us with the original context of this saying in the *Analects*.

V, 21   This saying exists in two forms. The version of the *Analects* reoccurs verbatim in the *Ju-lin Chuan* (ch. 121 of the *Shih Chi*) and, apart from the insertion of one superfluous character,[1] also in the Life of Confucius[2] (ch. 47 of the *Shih Chi*). But in another passage[3] of the Life and in *Mencius*[4] Confucius is made to say 'Let us return . . . the little ones . . . push themselves forward and grab' (the opposite of the essential principle *jang*: yield, give place to others). They cannot forget their beginnings' (i.e. they are always lapsing back into the old ways of greed and push that are inconsistent with my Way of Goodness).

V, 24   When later Confucians were attempting to make Confucius in some way responsible (either as author or editor) for the whole of early Chinese literature, they turned Tso Ch'iu Ming into a disciple of Confucius and credited him with the authorship (under the Master's direction) of the *Tso Chuan* chronicle. Nothing further is known about him.

VI, 6   *Ta* means 'to put through', 'penetrate'. So (1) To 'put oneself through', to turn one's *te* to account, to get on in the world, to progress; to get one's meaning or one's doctrines through, i.e. to 'put them across'. (2) To get through, penetrate, i.e. understand.

VI, 11   From the Han dynasty onwards the word *ju*, which is of very uncertain origin, was applied to those who devoted themselves to the study of the *Songs*, the *Books*, the ritual treatises, etc., and hence to followers of Confucius in general. It seems, however, to have originally been a contemptuous nickname given by the warlike people of

1   *Wu* (I) is inserted before 'do not know how to'; which does not make sense.
2   Chavannes' translation, V, p 359.
3   ibid. p. 343.
4   VII, B, 37.

Ch'i to their more pacific neighbours in Lu. cf. *Tso Chuan*, Ai kung, 21st year. But since the word occurs only this once in the *Analects*, without adequate context, it is impossible to know for certain what meaning the compilers attached to it.

VI, 21 This saying, in the form in which it now occurs, is completely Taoistic, save that the word Good (Goodness) has been substituted for 'Tao'. Taoism, it is true, drew its vocabulary and ideas partly from a stock common to all early Chinese thought. But nowhere else in the *Analects* is it suggested that anyone save the *Shêng* (Divine Sage) can achieve his ends by inactivity, and as this passage stands it is impossible not to give it a more general application. But comparison with other sayings in the *Analects* and elsewhere suggests that this saying originally had a very different form. In XV, 32, it is *shou* (keeping what one has gained) and not *shou* (longevity) which is the consequence of Goodness, but cannot result from wisdom alone. Moreover, in the *Ku-liang Chuan*[1] we twice get the saying 'The wise man schemes (*lü*) . . . the Good man keeps' ('secures', *shou*) what the scheming has achieved. Both passages are concerned with politics, not with the moral life of the individual, and mean that State successes gained by cleverness will not be permanent; only the State that is based on Goodness can have any permanence.

As it stands, the saying runs very awkwardly. It is first said that the Good man delights (*lo*) in mountains and then that it is the wise man who 'delights'; whereas the Good man is 'long-lived' (*shou*) as opposed to 'delighting' (*lo*). I cannot help believing that the original sense of the last two phrases was: 'The wise ruler schemes; but the Good ruler alone can give permanent effect to schemes', as in the *Ku-liang Chuan*.

The Good 'stay still', because their effects are achieved by *te* (moral force) not by *li* (physical force). The dictum

1 Yin 2 and Huan 18.

easily passes into the vocabulary of full-blown, systematic quietism.

Pao Hsien, in the first century, takes the whole saying as referring to the ruler. But it is usually taken to refer to the individual in general, and is interpreted in a completely Taoist sense: all exercise of the emotions destroys the soul and leads to early death.

VI, 26   'Made a solemn declaration', literally 'arrowed it'. Here metaphorical; but probably the character 'arrow' has its ideogrammatic sense and is not a phonetic substitute. For the use of a bundle of arrows in oath-taking, see H. Maspero (Mélanges chinois et bouddhiques, III, p. 270). *Le Serment dans la procédure judiciaire* . . . The bundle of arrows is a symbol of the unbreakable, in contrast with a single arrow, that can easily be snapped. cf. the memorial inscription of the Mongol leader Mêng-ku (13th century) by Yao Sui[1] (AD 1238–1314): He broke an arrow and swore saying: 'May every act in which I am not utterly faithful to the Khan be snapped like this!' We see here that it is against his acts and not against himself that the speaker invokes destruction. Confucius's *yeh chih* is generally translated 'crush (reject, forsake) me'. But the text says 'it' not 'me', following a formula similar to that of the Mongol oath. There is no evidence that *yeh* can mean 'reject'. Nor is there any suggestion in the text that improper conduct had taken place between Nan-tzu and Confucius, but only that his seeing her at all, as a means of obtaining influence at the Wei Court, was improper.

VI, 27   It is upon this passage that the whole Confucian philosophy of compromise, of 'too much is as bad as too little', is built. What *chung-yung* meant to start with is very doubtful. To the compilers of the *Analects*, I do not think it meant anything different from *chung tao*, the Middle Way. But the interpretation 'middle and usual', i.e. 'traditional', is a quite possible one.

A Confucian treatise of very mixed content, strongly

1   Collected Works, XIV, I verso.

tinged with Taoism, deals in several passages with the power of *chung-yung*, and bears these two words as its title. (It is known in Europe as the *Doctrine of the Mean*.) The material that this treatise contains is partly, at any rate, as old as the first half of the third century; but the unification of China is referred to, and the actual compilation of the work must be as late as the end of the third century BC.

Is there not, however, some connection between this passage and *Song* 142, which recounts the virtues of Chung Shan Fu? The 6th verse says: 'Moral force (*te*) is light as a hair; but among the people there are few that can lift it' (i.e. that can use it).

I suspect that in its original form the saying was parallel to that about T'ai Po in VIII, 1, and ran: 'How transcendent was the *te* of Chung Shan Fu (Minister of King Hsüan of Chou). That among the people there are few (who know how to use *te*) is an old story!' in allusion to *Song* 142, verse 6. The two characters *shan* and *fu*, written too close one above the other, were later misread as a single character *yung*. This however is merely a tentative suggestion.

VII, 7   As in modern Chinese school-fees are called 'the bundle of dried flesh,' it would not occur to the average reader that *shu-hsiu* in this passage could possibly mean anything but 'a bundle of dried flesh,' brought as a humble present to the teacher. This, however, was not the view of many outstanding commentators. Chêng Hsüan (died AD 200) says it means 'fourteen years old': the Master accepted any pupil who had attained to years of discretion. The alternatives arise in this way: *Shu* = to tie, tie one's belt. *Hsiu* = 'to put right', 'to cure'; hence to 'cure' meat, so that 'tied cured' means 'a bundle of dried flesh' or one who has 'tied his belt and put himself to rights', i.e. has donned the garb of manhood. There is, however, no trace of this idiom till Han times; whereas 'dried flesh', as a humble form of offering, occurs in texts which have every chance of being pre-Han. I therefore think that Huang K'an (sixth century) was right in championing the 'dried flesh' theory against the view of Chêng Hsüan.

VII, 17   There is not much doubt that *ya* (refined, standard, correct as applied to speech) is etymologically the same word as the ethnic term Hsia, the common name of the Chinese, as opposed to the barbarians. Mo Tzu calls the third part of the *Book of Songs* 'Ta Hsia' instead of the usual *Ta Ya*.[1]

To avoid the implication that Confucius sometimes spoke in his native dialect, Ch'êng Hao in the eleventh century interpreted *ya* as meaning not 'standard', but 'standardly', i.e. frequently. Hence Legge's 'His frequent themes were . . .' But Chêng Hsüan interprets the passage exactly as I have done.

VII, 18   It is the 'Duke' of Shê who is the subject of the following anecdote. There was once a man who said he had a passion for dragons. He was always talking about them, and had them painted all over the walls of his house. After all, he said, there is nothing pleasanter to look at than a dragon. One day a huge, shiny, slimy paw flopped on to his window-sill; soon a green and golden scaly face reared itself up at the window and grinned a dank greeting. The lover of dragons was beside himself with terror. He fled shrieking to the hall, where he tripped over the oozing, slithery tail which the monster had thrust in friendly salutation through the doorway of the house.

The story is told as a warning against insincere enthusiasms. (See Waley, *Introduction to the Study of Chinese Painting*, p. 37.)

VIII, 3   The passage quoted from the *Li Chih I* refers, it must be admitted, to the death of an emperor, not a private person.

Trussing up of various kinds and the placing of heavy weights on the body occur in many parts of the world, in some cases before death, in some cases after it. Where such practices take place after death, they are explained by anthropologists as being due to fear of the dead returning

---

1   The variant has been smoothed away from Mo Tzu's text by modern editors.

to life.[1] Where they occur before death this explanation obviously does not hold good. The question is complicated by the fact that in China (and probably elsewhere?) many practices originally belonging to the period preceding death were in less primitive days delayed until death had actually taken place; see De Groot, *The Religious Systems of China*, I, p. 9.

VIII, 15   The interpretation of *shih* (began) as 'when he first entered on his duties' seems to date from Sung times.

VIII, 20   King Wu's statement that he had 'ten ministers' is found in several passages of old literature; e.g. *Tso Chuan*, Duke Hsiang, 28th year.[2]

IX, 2   The commentators take the villager's 'vastly learned', etc. not as irony but as praise; for to achieve a reputation in any one line is unworthy of a *chün-tzu*. This seems to make Confucius's comment unintelligible. I take the villager to be a boorish, ignorant man who does not know that a true gentleman ought not to be known as a specialist in any one line.

IX, 5   The people of K'uang are supposed to have mistaken Confucius for the adventurer Yang Huo (see XVII, 1) who had formerly created a disturbance in K'uang. The mistake was made more natural by the fact that Confucius's carriage was being driven by a man who had previously been associated with Yang Huo.

X, 10   For the No (expulsion rite) see *Chou Li*, ch. 48 and 54. The exorcist accompanied by four 'Madmen' (see *The Book of Songs*, p. 222) 'wearing over their heads a bear's skin with four eyes of yellow metal (copper or gold?), clad in a black

1   cf. Frazer, *The Fear of the Dead in Primitive Religion*, 2 vols., 1933 and 1934.
2   The omission of the word 'ministers' in some early versions (e.g. the T'ang Scriptures on Stone) was a doctrinal not a philological emendation. It is unfilial to speak of a mother as being 'minister' (literally 'servant') to her son.

coat and red skirt, grasping halberd and raising shield, leads all the house-servants and performs the No of the season, searching the house and driving out noxious influences.'

In many parts of Europe the whole household still visits every corner of the house and outbuildings on New Year's Eve, banging forks on dish-covers and so on, in order to drive out the Old Year.

The *Chi Chieh* says that Confucius stood on the eastern steps of the ancestral shrine during this ceremony 'in order to reassure the ancestral spirits' of the house, who might otherwise have taken flight along with the 'noxious influences'. In T'ang times the No was stylised as a Court dance.

XI, 4   Min Tzu-ch'ien's mother died when he was a child and his father married again. One day when he was driving his father's carriage he let the reins slip. His father found that he was wearing such thin gloves that his hands were numbed with cold. On going home he looked at the gloves worn by the two children born to him by his second wife and found that they were thick and warm. He said to his wife, 'I married you solely in order to have someone to look after my motherless children. Now I can see that you have been imposing upon me. Leave my home at once!' Tzu-ch'ien said, 'If my stepmother remains, one child will be imperfectly clad; but if she goes, several children will be cold.' His father said no more about it. (Fragment of lost portions of *Shuo Yüan*, quoted under heading 'filial piety' in *I Wên Lei Chü*.)

XI, 7   *Kuo* (the word translated 'enclosure') meant, as may be seen most clearly from the paragraph on 'Inspecting the *kuo* and grave-figures' in *I Li*, XII, a protection for the coffin made by laying beams longways and crossways, like the framework at the top of a well. Excavation has confirmed this; cf. S. Umehara, *Selected Relics from the Chin-ts'un Tombs*, Lo-yang. Kyoto, 1937, Fig. 3.

In later times *kuo* meant an 'outer coffin', a 'shell'. In Japan the term 'stone *kuo*' has been applied to the *allées couvertes* of Japanese megalithic structures.

XI, 13   Duke Chao, who fled from Lu in 517 BC, had used this building as a basis for operations against his enemies, the Chi Family. It is probable, therefore, that the remark of Min Tzu-ch'ien was applauded by Confucius for its loyalist, pro-dynastic tendency.

XI, 24   For the Holy Ground, see additional note to III, 21. The Millet is in early texts always closely associated with the Holy Ground and not treated as the object of a separate cult.[1] It was interpreted as symbolising the fruits of the soil in general. It was no doubt a sheaf of millet (if grain had been meant another word would have been used) and may have been the Last Sheaf, kept over from the previous harvest. 'Last Sheaf' ceremonies are common in India, Indo-China and Indonesia.

XI, 25, 7   The ritualists describe four rain-ceremonies, one for each season. But there is reason to believe[2] that the ceremony carried out at the end of spring or beginning of summer and traceable throughout Chinese history down to the present day is the only one that has, as a regular institution, had any real existence. During times of drought an emergency ceremony might indeed be performed; but the four ceremonies, each corresponding to a season, a colour, etc., are a pure fantasy of the ritualists.

    A constant feature of these ceremonies is, as Professor Shiratori has shown, the participation of boys and young men.

    5 x 6 + 6 x 7 makes 72, a number used in other dances.[3] The performance of lustrations preceded every sacrifice, and there is not the slightest reason to emend the character

---

1   'The *Chi (Millet)* is a detail of the *shê*', as Chêng Hsüan puts it, in commenting on *Chou Li*, XXII.

2   See K. Shiratori, *Tōyō Gakuhō*, XXI, 2, pp. 104 seq.

3   e.g. the dance to Hou Chi, the god of agriculture, which was performed by 'capped youths five times six which is thirty, and boys six times seven which is forty-two.' See *Han Ch'iu I*, quoted among the fragments collected in *P'ing Ching Kuan Ts'ung Shu*, Supplement, ch. 2, fol. 6.

yü 'bathe', on the ground that the season was too cold for bathing (cf. *Lun Hêng*, P'ien 45, fol. 11).

The commentator quoted by the *Lun Hêng* (first century AD) is trying to explain this passage in the light of the popular rain-ceremonies held in his own day, and I do not think we can accept his interpretation in all its details.[1] The whole of this very literary passage bears the stamp of belonging to a milieu different from that of the brief colloquial sayings. It is noteworthy that *an* (usual sense 'peaceful') is used as an interrogative particle.[2] This usage does not seem to belong either to the older language (only one very doubtful example occurs in the *Songs*) or to the language of Lu (no other example in the *Lun Yü*; none in *Mencius*). On the other hand, it is extremely common in the (more northerly?) dialect of the *Tso Chuan*, and in third century BC writings generally.

XII, 20   *lü i hsia jen.* cf. *Tso Chuan*, Hsüan Kung 12th year, 'A people whose prince knows how to defer to others (*nêng i hsia jen*) may be treated as reliable.' *lü* sometimes means 'in general', 'on the whole'. (See Wang Nien-sun, *Tu Shu Tsa Chih* VIII, 4 and Yü Yüeh, H. P. 1392, fol. 7.) I doubt if that is the sense here.

XIII, 3   For *kou* (chance) see *Han Shih Wai Chuan*, III, fol. 1 and IV, fol. 1 verso. Also *Tso Chuan*, Chao Kung, 18th year. It is used when things are done 'somehow or other', in a 'hit or miss' offhand fashion, when everything is 'left to chance'. In hypothetical clauses it means 'If by any chance', 'If somehow or other'. It applies wherever a result is achieved by mere accident and not as the result of *te* (virtue, moral power). cf. XIII, 8.

XIII, 4   Confucius took the traditional view that it is for common people to work with their hands, for gentlemen to work

---

1   cf. M. Granet, *Fêtes et Chansons Anciennes de la Chine*, 1929, p. 158.
2   But the text used by Lu Tê-ming seems to have had the usual particle *yen*.

with their *te*. Fan Ch'ih had evidently been influenced by views similar to those of Hsü Hsing (*Mencius*, III, A, 4) who held that it was unfair to live by the labour of others and maintained that 'the wise man should plough side by side with the common people'. There is a parallel passage in *Mo Tzu* (Lu Wên, P'ien, 49), where 'a low fellow, from the south of Lu, called Wu Lü', reproaches Mo Tzu with preaching justice, while all the time living on the labour of others. Mo Tzu's reply amounts practically to saying that he is promoting justice more by teaching it to others than he would be by practising it himself.

XIII, 15   Wang Su (died AD 256), Huang K'an (died AD 545) and Hsing P'ing (died AD 1010) all accept that *chi* (current interpretation 'expect', 'count upon) means 'near'. Chu Hsi bases his 'expect' on an isolated and very uncertain usage in *Song* 199.

XIII, 22   It seems clear that *hêng* was the name of a ritual. cf. *Chou Li*, ch. 50: 'If a great calamity befalls the land, then send for *wu* (shamans) and perform the *wu-hêng* (shamanistic *hêng* ceremony).' The explanations given by Chêng Hsüan and other *Chou Li* commentators are forced and unconvincing. *Mo Tzu* (XXXII, Forke's translation, p. 371) quotes from a 'book of the former kings': 'to perform the *hêng* dance in the palace is called yielding to the influence of shamans.' To dance *hêng* 'continually' (which is the usual interpretation) makes poor sense. I would also suggest that the words 'ill, *hêng*, not die' in the *Book of Changes*, section 16, mean 'If anyone is ill, perform the *hêng* rite and he will not die.' The saying of the 'men of the south' (i.e. of Ch'u?) is also quoted in Section 32 of the *Changes*.

XIV, 16   The usual interpretation, 'Wên was crafty and not upright, Huan was upright and not crafty' is, as Wang Nien-sun long ago observed (*Ching I Shu Wên*, on this passage), nonsensical. The story of Wên (Double Ears,[1] as he was

---

1   Like many heroes, he was noted for strange physical peculiarities; his ribs were all in one piece.

called) is known to us chiefly through a heroic legend embodied in *Kuo Yü,* IX and X. The commentators try to discover a lack of ritual correctness in the story of his being visited by the Divine King (T'ien-wang, i.e. the ruler of Chou). But this requires some ingenuity. We only know a legend that praises him; we must suppose Confucius to have known one which denigrated him.

Of Duke Huan's failure in emergencies no convincing example is cited. For this sense of *chüeh,* see Liu Pao-nan's *Lun Yü Chêng I.*

XIV, 33   Usually taken as meaning 'who does not anticipate deceit . . . and, yet immediately perceives it when it occurs.' There are two objections to this rendering: (1) The *i* of *pu hsin, i* . . . usually means 'or', not 'but'; (2) *hsien chüeh* normally means to perceive beforehand, not 'to perceive immediately', and the text says nothing about 'when it has occurred', or the like. Confucius is criticising a current maxim about the *chün-tzu.*

XV, 10   The tunes of Chêng and Wei are often referred to as 'new music' or the 'common music of the world'. Towards classical music, the 'music of the former Kings' (*Mencius,* I, B, 2) ordinary as opposed to serious-minded people had the same feelings as they have towards our own classical music to-day. 'How is it', the Prince of Wei asked Tzu-hsia, 'that when I sit listening to old music, dressed in my full ceremonial gear, I am all the time in terror of dropping off asleep; whereas when I listen to the tunes of Chêng and Wei, I never feel the least tired?' (*Li Chi,* XIX, fol. 5).

XV, 25   The current interpretation is 'lent it to others to drive'.[1] This gives a sense totally unconnected with what goes before. Moreover, *chieh jen* occurs elsewhere[2] in the sense 'to avail oneself of the services of others', but never is the

---

1   'To ride' is an anachronism; for horses were not ridden in the time of Confucius.

2   *Tso Chuan,* Hsiang Kung, 19th year; and *Kuan Tzu,* P'ien 33, *chieh jen,* 'set other people to do it for you'.

sense 'to lend to others'. *Chieh* in the sense 'to lend' is very rare in early texts, while in the sense 'to borrow' it is very common.

XVI, 14   It will be noticed that although the words *jen* (person) and *chün* (prince), here applied to a lady, are not exclusively masculine, they are chiefly and prevailingly applied to men rather than to women. For example, in VIII, 20, Confucius says that King Wu had not really 'ten *jen*' to help him; for one of them was a woman. *Hsiao T'ung* (Little boy) means a pageboy, and is an exclusively masculine term. Thus it may be said that the sovereign's wife may not be referred to (either by himself or anyone else) by any term that is feminine in implication and must in referring to herself use a term that is definitely masculine.

This is in obedience to the general principle that a sovereign must be spoken of as though he were free from ordinary human needs and desires.[1] It will also be noted that the sovereign speaks of himself as the 'lonely one'. This he does under all circumstances, and not only in reference to his wife. Thus his city is 'the lonely one's city', etc. In China he was 'lonely' in the sense that his father, whose throne he had inherited, was necessarily dead. But a king is often technically motherless as well as fatherless. For at his accession he must either, as in some parts of the world, marry his mother, and so lose her as a mother; or else 'never set eyes on his mother'.[2] Or again, his mother has been ritually sacrificed during the funeral ceremony of his father. It is possible that the expression 'the lonely one' goes back in China to times when the king was technically motherless as well as fatherless.

XX, 1   *T'ien chih li-shu* was no doubt understood in a quasi-abstract sense by the compilers of the *Analects:* 'Heaven's succession', i.e. the succession accorded by Heaven. It is

1   cf. C. G. Seligman, *Egypt and Negro Africa, a Study in Divine Kingship,* 1934, p. 47.
2   op. cit., p. 43.

possible, however, that in its original setting, as a formula used in the accession-rites of kings, it had a much more concrete sense: 'The calendar[1] and counting-sticks of Heaven' (i.e. of the Ancestors).

There is a hiatus after 'his charge to Yü'. In other Chinese works (e.g. in the forged portions of the *Shu Ching*, in *Mo tzu* and in the *Kuo Yü*) many of the sentences strung together in this paragraph will be found utilised for a different purpose and interpreted with a different meaning. A discussion of all these parallels belongs rather to the textual criticism of the *Shu Ching* than to a study of the *Analects*, and I shall not attempt it here.

The Ku version treated XX, 2 and 3 as a separate book.

---

1   i.e. 'succession' of agricultural tasks.

WORDSWORTH CLASSICS
OF WORLD LITERATURE

APULEIUS
The Golden Ass

ARISTOTLE
The Nicomachean Ethics

MARCUS AURELIUS
Meditations

FRANCIS BACON
Essays

JOHN BUNYAN
The Pilgrim s Progress

KARL VON CLAUSEVITZ
On War (ABRIDGED)

CONFUCIUS
The Analects

CHARLES DARWIN
The Voyage of the Beagle

RENÉ DESCARTES
*A Discourse on Method
& other Essays*

SIGMUND FREUD
The Interpretation of Dreams

EDWARD GIBBON
*The Decline and Fall of the
Roman Empire* (ABRIDGED)

KHALIL GIBRAN
The Prophet

HERODOTUS
The Histories

HORACE
Selected Odes

LAO TSU
Tao te Ching

T. E. LAWRENCE
Seven Pillars of Wisdom

SIR THOMAS MALORY
Le Morte Darthur

JOHN STUART MILL
*On Liberty & The Subjection
of Women*

SIR THOMAS MORE
Utopia

THOMAS PAINE
Rights of Man

MARCO POLO
Travels

SAMUEL PEPYS
Selections from the Diary

PLATO
*The Symposium &
The Death of Socrates
The Republic*

LA ROCHEFOUCAULD
Maxims

JEAN-JACQUES ROUSSEAU
The Confessions

SUETONIUS
The Twelve Caesars

THUCYDIDES
*The History of the
Peloponnesian War*